Employment
Development
Department
State of California

2024 CALIFORNIA EMPLOYER'S GUIDE

Important Information

Effective January 1, 2024, Senate Bill 951 removes the taxable wage limit and maximum withholdings for each employee subject to State Disability Insurance (SDI) contributions.

Electronic Reporting and Payment Requirement: All employers must electronically submit employment tax returns, wage reports, and payroll tax deposits to the Employment Development Department (EDD). For more information, visit E-file and E-pay mandate (edd.ca.gov/EfileMandate) or refer to page 49.

e-Services for Business: Employers can file, pay, and manage their employer payroll tax account online. For more information, visit e-Services for Business (edd.ca.gov/eServices) or refer to page 50.

State Information Data Exchange System (SIDES): Employers and third-party administrators can elect to electronically receive and respond to the EDD *Notice of Unemployment Insurance Claim Filed* (DE 1101CZ) using SIDES. For more information, visit SIDES (edd.ca.gov/SIDES).

New Employee Registry (NER): All employers are required by law to report all newly hired or rehired employees to the NER within 20 days of their start-of-work date. For more information, visit NER California's New Hire Reporting Program (edd.ca.gov/Payroll_Taxes/New_Hire_Reporting.htm) or refer to page 53.

Payroll Tax Seminars: The EDD offers no-cost seminars to help employers comply with state payroll tax laws. For more information, visit Payroll Tax Seminars (edd.ca.gov/payroll_tax_seminars) or refer to page 1.

Fraud Prevention, Detection, and Reporting: For information on how to prevent and detect fraud, visit Help Fight Fraud (edd.ca.gov/about_edd/fraud.htm). Refer to page 83 for information about UI fraud, or page 95 for DI fraud.

Improper Payment of UI Benefits: When an employer is financially impacted by improper UI payments, the problem can result in higher UI taxes for all employers. You can help by responding timely to requests for wage information. For more information, visit UI claim notices (edd.ca.gov/unemployment/responding_to_ui_claim_notices.htm).

California Employer News and Updates: Find the latest tax news, annual updates, and resources to support you and your business. Visit Employer News and Updates (edd.ca.gov/payroll_taxes/employer-news.htm) and subscribe to receive emails about employment and payroll tax updates.

2024 Payroll Tax Rates, Taxable Wage Limits, and Maximum Benefit Amounts

Unemployment Insurance (UI)

- The 2024 taxable wage limit is $7,000 per employee.
- The UI maximum weekly benefit amount is $450.
- The UI tax rate for new employers is 3.4 percent (.034) for a period of two to three years.
- The employer rates are available online at e-Services for Business (edd.ca.gov/eServices).

Employment Training Tax (ETT)

- The 2024 ETT rate is 0.1 percent (.001) on the first $7,000 of each employee's wages.

State Disability Insurance (SDI)

- The 2024 SDI withholding rate is 1.1 percent (.011). The rate includes Disability Insurance (DI) and Paid Family Leave (PFL).
- There is no SDI taxable wage limit beginning January 1, 2024. DI and PFL maximum weekly benefit amount are available online at Quick Statistics (edd.ca.gov/en/about_edd/quick_statistics).

California Personal Income Tax (PIT) Withholding

California PIT withholding is based on the amount of wages paid, the number of withholding allowances claimed by the employee, and the payroll period.

For additional information on PIT withholding refer to pages 15 and 17 or visit Rates and Withholding (edd.ca.gov/payroll_taxes/rates_and_withholding.htm).

EDD Employment Development Department
State of California

Dear California Employer:

The Employment Development Department (EDD) understands your time is valuable. We are committed to providing you with the tools and resources to manage your payroll tax account online.

We've made it easier to file and pay with e-Services for Business (edd.ca.gov/eServices), available 24 hours a day, 7 days a week. You can file, adjust, print returns, make payments, update your account information, and much more!

The EDD has recently streamlined our website, creating a more functional and user-friendly experience, including a virtual agent who can help answer common questions. We encourage you to explore our improved EDD website (edd.ca.gov) to learn more about many of our programs and services. As a valued employer, we have a Payroll Taxes (edd.ca.gov/Payroll_Taxes) resource page to help you understand your California payroll tax reporting responsibilities. You can also register for Payroll Tax Seminars (edd.ca.gov/payroll_tax_seminars) at no-cost to help established employers and new employers understand and comply with state payroll tax laws.

Join the many employers taking advantage of going paperless, to save time and space, while helping to preserve the environment. You can access the *California Employer's Guide* (DE 44) at (edd.ca.gov/en/Payroll_Taxes/Employers_Guides). If you're currently receiving a paper guide, you can opt-out on e-Services for Business.

Take advantage of our email subscription service (edd.ca.gov/about_edd/get_email_notices.htm) and receive the latest updates, reminders, and information on our programs and services.

We are available and stand ready to answer your payroll tax questions, contact our Taxpayer Assistance Center at 1-888-745-3886.

We wish you continued success in the year ahead.

Sincerely,

NANCY FARIAS
Director

PO Box 826880 • Sacramento, CA 94280-0001 • edd.ca.gov

Manage Your Employer Payroll Tax Account Online!

Use e-Services for Business to electronically:

- File tax returns and wage reports
- Make payments
- Update addresses
- And much more

Enroll at e-Services for Business
(edd.ca.gov/eServices).

You can view or download this
guide at California Employer Guides
(edd.ca.gov/en/Payroll_Taxes/Employers_Guides).

Seminars to Help Employers Succeed

We offer no-cost seminars to help employers understand and comply with California's payroll tax laws.

EDD offers seminars on the following topics:	
• State payroll tax reporting requirements and recordkeeping. • Federal and State Basic Payroll Tax Seminar. • State Labor Law and Payroll Tax Seminar.	• Employment Status Tax Seminar. • Cannabis Industry and State Payroll Tax Seminar. • AB 5 Motor Carrier Worker Classification Online Webinar.
EDD and the Internal Revenue Service (IRS) jointly offer seminars on:	**EDD and the Department of Industrial Relations' Division of Labor Standards Enforcement jointly present classes on:**
• Federal and state payroll reporting and withholding requirements. • Difference between employees and independent contractors and the importance of proper worker classification.	• Wage and hour laws and regulations. • Employer and employee rights and responsibilities. • Recordkeeping, reporting, and posting requirements.

Register for a tax seminar at Payroll Tax Seminar
(edd.ca.gov/payroll_tax_seminars).

Go Paperless!
You can view or download this guide at
California Employer Guides
(edd.ca.gov/en/Payroll_Taxes/Employers_Guides).

Introduction

This guide helps you understand your rights and responsibilities as an employer.

How to Use This Guide

This guide provides information you need to know as an employer, such as when to register, how to determine who is an employee, what are wages, payment and posting requirements. Find the topics you need in the table of contents then review the information and web resources provided for additional information.

The Employment Development Department (EDD) administers payroll tax reporting laws according to the California Unemployment Insurance Code (CUIC) and Labor Code (LC). Regardless of the size of your business, this guide is an important resource on the procedures required for compliance with California payroll tax laws. This guide will help clarify how the CUIC and California Code of Regulations (CCR) impact your business. We follow federal tax guidelines and due dates. However, California laws and rates may differ from federal laws and rates.

This guide provides general information that applies to most employers and references information on specialized topics. Information on detailed or complex issues applicable to a small number of employers is not included.

How to Obtain Assistance and Additional Information

If you have questions not addressed in this guide and/or need additional information, visit the EDD (edd.ca.gov) website or contact the Taxpayer Assistance Center at 1-888-745-3886.

We offer seminars and presentations on California payroll tax reporting requirements to help you:

- Understand your California payroll tax reporting requirements.
- Avoid common pitfalls and costly mistakes.
- Learn the differences between employees and independent contractors.
- Understand your reporting requirements for new employees and independent contractors.
- Discover no-cost services and resources available to you.
- Develop a better understanding of the State Disability Insurance (SDI) program.

For additional information about a payroll tax education event near you, contact the Taxpayer Assistance Center at 1-888-745-3886 or register for a Payroll Tax Seminar (edd.ca.gov/payroll_tax_seminars).

Learn more about SDI educational presentations for California workers, military family members, employers, and licensed health professionals by visiting Outreach Events Information (edd.ca.gov/disability/events_calendar.htm) or emailing the SDI Outreach Development Section at diboutreach@edd.ca.gov

Other Services

This guide also contains useful information about our services specifically for employers including programs offering tax credits. We also provide employment services, such as job development and job search workshops, designed to reduce unemployment and your taxes. A variety of services for new and established employers can help you in building a more successful business while complying with California laws.

We Want to Hear From You

How can we improve this guide to better meet your needs? You may send your comments and suggestions to:

Employment Development Department
Publications and Marketing Services Group, MIC 93
PO Box 826880
Sacramento, CA 94280-0001

Email: pmsg@edd.ca.gov

Other Website of Interest

taxes.ca.gov – This website is sponsored by the California Department of Tax and Fee Administration, the EDD, the Franchise Tax Board, and the Internal Revenue Service (IRS).

Payroll Tax Help, Forms, and Publications

e-Services for Business

- Fulfills the e-file and e-pay mandate.
- Manage your employer payroll tax account online.
- Register as an employer.
- File tax returns and wage reports.
- Pay deposits and liabilities.
- Make address changes.

Register online using e-Services for Business, (edd.ca.gov/eServices).

Online

Visit the EDD (edd.ca.gov) website.

- Frequently asked questions (edd.ca.gov/payroll_taxes/faqs.htm).
- Payroll Tax Seminars (edd.ca.gov/payroll_tax_seminars).
- Tax Professionals (edd.ca.gov/payroll_taxes/tax_practitioners.htm).
- Ask EDD (askedd.edd.ca.gov).

Visit California Tax Service Center (taxes.ca.gov) for federal and California tax information for businesses and individuals.

Phone

Toll-free from the U.S. or Canada: 1-888-745-3886

Hearing impaired: 1-800-547-9565

Outside the U.S. or Canada: 1-916-464-3502

Staff are available from 8 a.m. to 5 p.m., Pacific Time, Monday through Friday to answer your questions.

Walk-In Offices

For information and advice on your payroll tax responsibilities, visit your local Employment Tax Office from 8 a.m. to 5 p.m., Pacific Time, Monday through Friday.

Anaheim................ 2099 S. State College Blvd., Suite 401, 92806
Audit and Collection Office Phone Number: 1-888-745-3886

Fresno.................. 1050 O Street, 93721
Audit Office Phone Number: 1-888-745-3886

Oakland................. 7677 Oakport Street, Suite 400, 94621
Audit Office Phone Number: 1-888-745-3886
Collection Office Phone Number: 1-888-745-3886

Redding................. 1325 Pine Street, 96001
Audit Office Phone Number: 1-888-745-3886

Sacramento .... 3321 Power Inn Road, Suite 220, 95826
Audit Office Phone Number: 1-888-745-3886
Collection Office Phone Number: 1-888-745-3886

San Bernardino...... 658 East Brier Drive, Suite 300, 92408
Audit Office Phone Number: 1-888-745-3886
Collection Office Phone Number: 1-888-745-3886

San Diego .... 10636 Scripps Summit Ct., Suite 202, 92131
Audit Office Phone Number: 1-888-745-3886

San Jose .... 906 Ruff Drive, 95110
Audit Office Phone Number: 1-888-745-3886

Santa Fe Springs... 10330 Pioneer Blvd., Suite 150, 90670
Audit Office Phone Number: 1-888-745-3886
Collection Office Phone Number: 1-888-745-3886

Van Nuys .... 6150 Van Nuys Blvd., Room 210, 91401
Audit Office Phone Number: 1-888-745-3886

To find an office near you, visit the Office Locator (edd.ca.gov/Office_Locator).

Self-Service Offices

Tax forms and free direct-line phones are available from 8 a.m. to 5 p.m., Pacific Time, Monday through Friday at our self-service offices.

Bakersfield........... 1800 30th Street, Suite 240, 93301
Modesto.............. 3340 Tully Road, Suite E-10, 95350
San Francisco ..... 745 Franklin Street, Suite 400, 94102
Santa Rosa.......... 50 D Street, Suite 100, 95404
Vallejo .... 1440 Marin Street, Suite 114, 94590
Ventura .... 4820 McGrath Street, Suite 200, 93003

Forms and Publications

Download and order forms, instructions, and publications at EDD Forms (edd.ca.gov/forms).

Quick and Easy Access for Tax Help, Forms, and Publications

Start Here

As a new employer, the following steps ensure you meet your employer reporting, and tax payment obligations. Keep in mind that your employer requirements may not be limited to information on this page. Refer to page 5 for a flowchart of these steps.

You are a subject employer if you pay wages for employment to one or more people in excess of $100 during any calendar quarter.

Note: If you pay wages to people who work in or around your home, you may be considered a household employer. Refer to page 7 for additional information or view the Household Employer's Guide (DE 8829) (edd.ca.gov/pdf_pub_ctr/de8829.pdf).

Register for an EDD employer payroll tax account number online at e-Services for Business (edd.ca.gov/eServices). **You must register with EDD within 15 days of becoming a subject employer.** A commercial employer is a business connected with commerce or trade, operating primarily for profit. We will assign you an eight-digit employer payroll tax account number to identify your business when reporting and paying payroll taxes. Include your employer payroll tax account number on all deposits, returns, and correspondence submitted to us. For additional information and registration options, refer to page 7.

Action Required:

- **Report new employees** using the online *Report of New Employee(s)* (DE 34) at e-Services for Business (edd.ca.gov/eServices) within 20 days of the employee's start-of-work date. All employees who are newly hired, rehired after a separation of at least 60 consecutive days, or returning to work from a furlough, separation, leave of absence without pay, or termination must be reported to us. If you acquire an ongoing business and employ any of the former owner's workers, these employees are considered new hires, and you must report them to the EDD's New Employee Registry (edd.ca.gov/en/Payroll_Taxes/New_Hire_Reporting). For additional information and available reporting methods for reporting new employees, refer to page 53.

- **Report independent contractor information** using the online *Report of Independent Contractor(s)* (DE 542) at e-Services for Business (edd.ca.gov/eServices) within 20 days of **either** paying an independent contractor $600 or more for services performed **or** entering into a contract for $600 or more, whichever is earlier. Independent contractor information must be reported to the EDD. For additional information and available reporting methods for independent contractor reporting, refer to page 55.

- **Provide your employees with pamphlets** on employee withholdings, Unemployment Insurance (UI), Disability Insurance (DI), and Paid Family Leave (PFL). For additional information on employee pamphlets, refer to page 72.

- **Post an employee notice** with UI, DI, and PFL claim and benefit information. This notice should be posted in a prominent location, easily seen by your employees. The appropriate notice will be sent to you after you register. For additional information on employee notices, refer to page 72.

Make your *Payroll Tax Deposits* (DE 88) payments for UI, Employment Training Tax (ETT), State Disability Insurance (SDI), and California Personal Income Tax (PIT) online at e-Services for Business (edd.ca.gov/eServices). Your SDI and PIT withholdings deposit due dates are based on your federal deposit schedule and requirement and the amount of accumulated PIT that you have withheld. Your UI and ETT payments are due quarterly. For additional information about deposit requirements, refer to pages 58 and 59.

File a *Quarterly Contribution Return and Report of Wages* (DE 9) online at e-Services for Business (edd.ca.gov/eServices) to reconcile the tax and withholding amounts with your DE 88 deposits for the quarter. Also, file a *Quarterly Contribution Return and Report of Wages (Continuation)* (DE 9C) to report total subject wages paid, PIT wages, and PIT withheld for each employee for the quarter.

These reports are due on January 1, April 1, July 1, and October 1 of each year. These reports must be submitted even if you have no payroll during a calendar quarter. For additional information and available filing options, refer to pages 62 and 63.

Note: Failure to complete the above steps on time may result in penalty and interest charges. For information on your federal employment tax reporting requirements, access the IRS (irs.gov) website or contact the IRS at 1-800-829-4933.

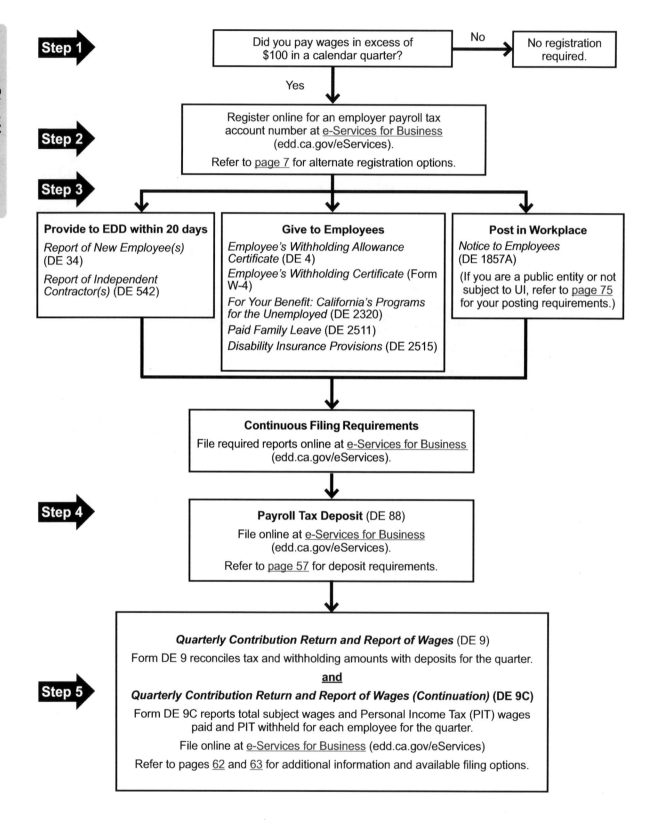

Start Here

Step 1 — Did you pay wages in excess of $100 in a calendar quarter?

No → No registration required.

Yes ↓

Step 2 — Register online for an employer payroll tax account number at e-Services for Business (edd.ca.gov/eServices).

Refer to page 7 for alternate registration options.

Step 3

Provide to EDD within 20 days
Report of New Employee(s) (DE 34)
Report of Independent Contractor(s) (DE 542)

Give to Employees
Employee's Withholding Allowance Certificate (DE 4)
Employee's Withholding Certificate (Form W-4)
For Your Benefit: California's Programs for the Unemployed (DE 2320)
Paid Family Leave (DE 2511)
Disability Insurance Provisions (DE 2515)

Post in Workplace
Notice to Employees (DE 1857A)
(If you are a public entity or not subject to UI, refer to page 75 for your posting requirements.)

Continuous Filing Requirements
File required reports online at e-Services for Business (edd.ca.gov/eServices).

Step 4 — **Payroll Tax Deposit** (DE 88)
File online at e-Services for Business (edd.ca.gov/eServices).
Refer to page 57 for deposit requirements.

Step 5

Quarterly Contribution Return and Report of Wages (DE 9)
Form DE 9 reconciles tax and withholding amounts with deposits for the quarter.

and

Quarterly Contribution Return and Report of Wages (Continuation) (DE 9C)
Form DE 9C reports total subject wages and Personal Income Tax (PIT) wages paid and PIT withheld for each employee for the quarter.
File online at e-Services for Business (edd.ca.gov/eServices)
Refer to pages 62 and 63 for additional information and available filing options.

Most forms are available online at EDD (edd.ca.gov) or by calling the Taxpayer Assistance Center at 1-888-745-3886.

2024 Forms and Due Dates

Form	Name	Due
DE 1	*Commercial Employer Account Registration and Update Form* (If you are **not** a commercial employer, refer to page 7.)	**Within 15 calendar days** after paying more than $100 in wages during any calendar quarter.
DE 34	*Report of New Employee(s)*	**Within 20 days** of start-of-work date for new or rehired employees.
DE 542	*Report of Independent Contractor(s)*	**Within 20 days** of paying an independent contractor $600 or more or entering into a contract for $600 or more, whichever is earlier.

Report	Quarter	Due	Delinquent if Not Filed By[1]
DE 9/DE 9C	1st (January, February, March)	**April 1, 2024**	**April 30, 2024**
DE 9/DE 9C	2nd (April, May, June)	**July 1, 2024**	**July 31, 2024**
DE 9/DE 9C	3rd (July, August, September)	**October 1, 2024**	**October 31, 2024**
DE 9/DE 9C	4th (October, November, December)	**January 1, 2025**	**January 31, 2025**

California Deposit Requirements

If Your Federal Deposit Schedule/ Requirement Is[1]	And You Have Accumulated State PIT Withholding Of	If Pay Date Is	PIT and SDI Deposit Due by[2]	California *Deposit Schedule* box to indicate on the DE 88
Next-Day	Less than $350	Any payday	Quarterly[3]	Quarterly
	$350 to $500	Any payday	15th of the following month	Monthly
	More than $500	Any payday	Next-Day	Next-Day
Semi-weekly	Less than $350	Any payday	Quarterly[3]	Quarterly
	$350 to $500	Any payday	15th of the following month	Monthly
	More than $500	Wed., Thurs., or Fri.	Following Wednesday[7]	Semi-weekly
	More than $500	Sat., Sun., Mon., or Tues.	Following Friday[7]	Semi-weekly
Monthly	Less than $350	Any payday	Quarterly[3]	Quarterly
	$350 or more	Any payday	15th of the following month	Monthly
Quarterly[4, 5] or Annually[6]	Less than $350	Any payday	April 30, 2024 July 31, 2024 October 31, 2024 January 31, 2025	Quarterly
	$350 or more	Any payday	15th of the following month	Monthly

1. If the due date falls on a Saturday, Sunday, or legal holiday, the due date is extended to the next business day. For example, if a deposit is due on Friday, but Friday is a holiday, the deposit due date is extended to the following Monday.
2. Electronic transactions for Next-Day deposits must be settled in the state's bank account on or before the third business day following the payroll date.
3. If the due date falls on a Saturday, Sunday, or legal holiday, the due date is extended to the next business day. For example, if a deposit is due on Friday, but Friday is a holiday, the deposit due date is extended to the following Monday.
4. If you have accumulated less than $350 of Personal Income Tax (PIT) and you choose to make an additional deposit before the quarterly due date, designate the *deposit schedule* as *quarterly* on your DE 88.
5. If you are not required to follow one of the above federal deposit schedules/requirements, you are still required to make California payroll tax deposits of accumulated State Disability Insurance (SDI) deductions and PIT withholdings quarterly or more often, based on the guidelines in this table. Information about federal deposit schedules is located in the Internal Revenue Service's *Employer Tax Guide* (Publication 15).
6. A deposit of employer Unemployment Insurance (UI) and Employment Training Tax (ETT) taxes and any accumulated SDI and PIT withholdings not previously paid *must be deposited each quarter* by the due dates shown.
7. If your federal deposit requirement is annually, you are required to make California payroll tax deposits quarterly or monthly based on the guidelines in this table.

About Employers

An employer is a person or legal entity that hires one or more employees to work for a wage, salary, or other compensation. Employers include sole proprietors, partnerships, corporations, nonprofit organizations, charitable organizations, foundations, limited liability companies, limited liability partnerships, public entities, including state and federal agencies, schools, associations, trusts, estates, joint ventures, and Indian Tribes.

When Do I Become a Subject Employer?

You become a subject employer when you pay wages in excess of $100 during any calendar quarter to one or more employees. Wages are compensation for services performed, including, but not limited to, cash payments, commissions, bonuses, and the reasonable cash value of nonmonetary payments for services, such as meals and lodging. For additional information, refer to *What Are Wages?* on page 11.

Private households, local college clubs, and local chapters of fraternities and sororities that employ workers to perform household services are *household employers*. Additional information about household employment is available online at Household Employer (edd.ca.gov/payroll_taxes/household_employer.htm). You can also refer to the *Household Employer's Guide* (DE 8829) (PDF) (edd.ca.gov/pdf_pub_ctr/de8829.pdf) online or obtain a copy by contacting the Taxpayer Assistance Center at 1-888-745-3886.

Note: If you acquired an existing business, refer to *What Is a Successor Employer?* on page 71 for further details.

When to Register

All employers conducting business in California are subject to the employment tax laws of the California Unemployment Insurance Code (CUIC). Once a business hires an employee and pays wages in excess of $100 during any calendar quarter, the business is considered to be a subject employer and must register at e-Services for Business (edd.ca.gov/eServices) or submit a registration form to us within 15 days after paying wages.

Employers are responsible for reporting wages paid to their employees and paying Unemployment Insurance (UI) tax and Employment Training Tax (ETT) on those wages, as well as withholding and remitting State Disability Insurance (SDI) and Personal Income Tax (PIT) due on those wages.

Action Required: Register with the EDD for an employer payroll tax account number if you pay wages in excess of $100 during any calendar quarter to one or more employees.

How to Register for an EDD Employer Payroll Tax Account Number

> Register online using the EDD e-Services for Business (edd.ca.gov/eServices).

Additional Options for Registering for an Employer Payroll Tax Account Number

1. Select the appropriate registration form for your industry available at Forms and Publications (edd.ca.gov/payroll_taxes/forms_and_publications.htm). The registration forms available are:
   - *Commercial Employer Account Registration and Update Form* (DE 1)
   - *Agriculture Employer Account Registration and Update Form* (DE 1AG)
   - *Governmental Organizations, Public Schools, and Indian Tribes Registration and Update Form* (DE 1GS)
   - *Employers of Household Workers Registration and Update Form* (DE 1HW)
   - *Nonprofit Employers Registration and Update Form* (DE 1NP)
   - *Employers Depositing Only Personal Income Tax Withholding Registration and Update Form* (DE 1P)

2. Submit the completed registration form by mail or fax to the EDD:

   Employment Development Department
   Account Services Group, MIC 28
   PO Box 826880
   Sacramento, CA 94280-0001

   Fax: 1-916-654-9211

Remember:
- Employment occurs when an employer engages the services of an employee for pay.
- You become a subject employer when you pay wages over $100 during any calendar quarter to one or more employees.
- You must register with the EDD within 15 days of paying wages in excess of $100.
- Employers are responsible for reporting wages paid to employees and paying UI and ETT on the wages, as well as withholding and remitting SDI and PIT.

Classifying Employees

An **employee** includes all of the following:

- Any officer of a corporation.
- Any worker who is an employee under the ABC test or Borello test.
- Any worker whose services are specifically covered by law.

An employee may perform services on a temporary or less than full-time basis. The law does not exclude services from employment that are commonly referred to as day labor, part-time help, casual labor, temporary help, probationary, or outside labor.

ABC Test, Employee or Independent Contractor?

What Is the ABC Test?

Under section 621 (b) of the CUIC and section 2775 of the Labor Code, an individual providing labor or services for payment shall be considered an employee rather than an independent contractor unless the hiring entity demonstrates that all of the following are satisfied:

A. The individual is free from the control and direction of the hiring entity in connection with the performance of the work, both under the contract for the performance of the work and in fact.

B. The individual performs work that is outside the usual course of the hiring entity's business.

C. The individual is customarily engaged in an independently established trade, occupation, or business of the same nature as that involved in the work performed.

Note: California does not provide relief under the *Safe Harbor* provisions of the Internal Revenue Code. Therefore, it is important that workers are properly classified under the ABC test which determines employer-employee relationships.

How Can I Get Additional Information on This Topic?

Incorrectly classifying your workers can be a costly mistake. If you have incorrectly classified employees as independent contractors, you could be liable for back taxes, penalties, and interest. The following EDD resources can help you determine if you have correctly classified your workers:

- *Employment Determination Guide (DE 38) (PDF)* (edd.ca.gov/pdf_pub_ctr/de38.pdf) – Asks a series of *Yes* or *No* questions regarding your treatment of workers to help determine if a problem may exist and whether you need to seek additional guidance. The DE 38 is available to download online.

- *Determination of Employment Work Status for Purposes of State of California Employment Taxes and Personal Income Tax Withholding (DE 1870) (PDF)* (edd.ca.gov/pdf_pub_ctr/de1870.pdf) – Provides a series of questions regarding your relationship with your workers. Complete and return this form to the EDD for a written determination stating whether your workers are employees or independent contractors based on the facts that you provide. The DE 1870 is available to download online.

- Information Sheets – Provide general and industry-specific information. To obtain information sheets, visit Forms and Publications (edd.ca.gov/payroll_taxes/forms_and_publications.htm) or contact the Taxpayer Assistance Center at 1-888-745-3886.

- **Independent Contractor Information** – The *Frequently Asked Questions and Answers About the California Independent Contractor Reporting Law (DE 542FAQ) (PDF)* (edd.ca.gov/pdf_pub_ctr/de542faq.pdf) and *Independent Contractors Misconceptions Brochure (DE 573M) (PDF)* (edd.ca.gov/pdf_pub_ctr/de573m.pdf) provides detailed information and are available online to download.

- **Payroll Tax Seminars** – EDD offers no-cost seminars online to help employers comply with the California payroll tax laws. To enroll, visit Payroll Tax Seminars (edd.ca.gov/payroll_tax_seminars) or contact the Taxpayer Assistance Center at 1-888-745-3886.

Remember:

- An employee includes any officer of a corporation, a worker who is an employee under the ABC test, and a worker whose services are specifically covered by law. Refer to *Information Sheet: Types of Employment (DE 231TE) (PDF)* (edd.ca.gov/pdf_pub_ctr/de231te.pdf) for more information.
- An employee may perform services on a temporary or less than full-time basis.
- We have several resources available to help you correctly classify your workers.

State Payroll Taxes

The Employment Development Department (EDD) administers the following California payroll tax programs:

- Unemployment Insurance (UI) Tax
- Employment Training Tax (ETT)
- State Disability Insurance (SDI) Withholding
- California Personal Income Tax (PIT) Withholding

Note: Paid Family Leave (PFL) is a component of the SDI program.

UI and ETT are employer paid contributions. SDI and PIT are withheld from employee wages. Wages are generally subject to all four payroll taxes unless otherwise stated by law.

Unemployment Insurance Tax

What Is UI Tax?

The UI program was established as part of a national program administered by the U.S. Department of Labor under the Social Security Act. The UI program provides temporary payments to individuals who are unemployed through no fault of their own.

Who Pays It?

The UI program is funded through payroll taxes paid by the employer. Tax-rated employers pay a percentage on the first $7,000 in wages paid to each employee in a calendar year. The UI rate schedule and amount of taxable wages are determined annually. New employers pay 3.4 percent (.034) for a period of two to three years. The UI rate could increase to a maximum of 6.2 percent (.062) or decrease to a minimum of 1.5 percent (0.015) based on an employer's experience rating and the balance in the UI Fund. For a detailed explanation of the experience rating method, refer to *Information Sheet: California System of Experience Rating* (DE 231Z) (PDF) (edd.ca.gov/pdf_pub_ctr/de231z.pdf).

Government entities and certain nonprofit employers may elect the reimbursable method of financing UI in which they reimburse the UI Fund on a dollar-for-dollar basis for all benefits paid to their former employees.

Employment Training Tax

What Is ETT?

ETT provides funds to train employees in targeted industries to improve the competitiveness of California businesses. The ETT fund promotes a healthy labor market by helping California businesses invest in a skilled and productive workforce while developing the skills of new and incumbent workers.

Who Pays It?

ETT is an employer-paid tax. Employers are subject to pay 0.1 percent (.001) for ETT on the first $7,000 in wages paid to each employee in a calendar year. The tax rate is set by statute at 0.1 percent (.001) of UI taxable wages for employers with positive UI reserve account balances and subject to section 977(c) of the California Unemployment Insurance Code (CUIC). The maximum tax is $7 per employee per year ($7,000 x .001).

State Disability Insurance Tax

What Is SDI Tax?

SDI allows the Disability Fund to pay Disability Insurance (DI) and PFL benefits to eligible California workers. DI benefits are paid to eligible California workers who lose wages when they are unable to work due to a non-work-related illness, injury, or pregnancy.

PFL benefits are paid to eligible California workers who take time off work to care for a seriously ill child, parent, parent-in-law, grandparent, grandchild, sibling, spouse, or registered domestic partner. Benefits are also available to new parents who need time to bond with a new child entering the family by birth, adoption, or foster care placement. Benefits are also available to California workers who participate in a qualifying event because of a family member's spouse, registered domestic partner, parent, or child's military deployment to a foreign country.

Who Pays It?

The SDI program is funded through a payroll deduction from employees' wages. Employers withhold 1.1 percent (.011) for SDI on all subject wages paid to each employee in a calendar year. The SDI rates may change each year.

California Personal Income Tax

What Is California PIT?

California PIT is a tax levied on California residents' income and on income that California nonresidents derive from California. The EDD reports, collects, and enforces PIT withholding. Taxes collected from the Franchise Tax Board (FTB) and the EDD support California public services such as schools, public parks, roads, health, and human services.

Who Pays It?

California PIT is either withheld from employee wages based on the *Employee's Withholding Allowance Certificate* (DE 4) on file with their employer or is based on the supplemental tax rates, refer to page 15.

State Payroll Taxes

	Unemployment Insurance	Employment Training Tax	State Disability Insurance	California Personal Income Tax
Who Pays?	Employer	Employer	Employee (employer withholds from employee wages)	Employee (employer withholds from employee wages)
Taxable Wages	First $7,000 of subject wages per employee, per year.	First $7,000 of subject wages per employee, per year.	No limit.	No limit. Refer to PIT withholding (edd.ca.gov/payroll_taxes/rates_and_withholding.htm).
Tax Rate	New employer tax rate is 3.4 percent (.034) for a period of two to three years. Following this period, the tax rate is calculated annually based on each employer's previous experience and the condition of the UI Fund. The EDD notifies employers of their new rate each December.	Set by statute at 0.1 percent (.001) of UI taxable wages for employers with positive UI reserve account balances and employers subject to section 977(c) of the CUIC.	The 2024 SDI withholding rate is 1.1 percent (.011). The SDI tax rate is set by law and may change each year	Withheld based on the *Employee's Withholding Allowance Certificate* (DE 4).
Maximum Tax (Except when employer is subject to section 977[c] of the CUIC.)	$434 per employee, per year. (The amount has been calculated at the highest UI tax rate of 6.2 percent [$7,000 x .062].)	$7 per employee, per year ($7,000 x .001).	No maximum.	No maximum.

Note: Some types of employment are not subject to payroll taxes or PIT withholding. Refer to *Information Sheet: Types of Employment* (DE 231TE) (PDF) (edd.ca.gov/pdf_pub_ctr/de231te.pdf). Certain types of wages and benefits are not subject to payroll taxes. Refer to *Information Sheet: Types of Payments* (DE 231TP) (PDF) (edd.ca.gov/pdf_pub_ctr/de231tp.pdf). For additional assistance, contact the Taxpayer Assistance Center at 1-888-745-3886.

Help Us Fight Fraud

The *underground economy* refers to those individuals and businesses that deal in cash or use other schemes to conceal their activities and their true tax liability from government licensing, regulatory, and taxing agencies. The underground economy is also referred to as tax evasion, tax fraud, cash pay, tax gap, payments under-the-table and off-the-books. When businesses operate in the underground economy, they gain an unfair advantage over businesses that comply with the law because they do not pay workers' compensation insurance and state and federal payroll taxes. The EDD, in partnership with several other governmental agencies, follows leads and conducts on-site inspections of businesses throughout the state. Visit EDD Underground Economy Operations (UEO) programs (edd.ca.gov/payroll_taxes/underground_economy_operations.htm) to learn more.

To report businesses that are paying workers undocumented cash payments, failing to carry workers' compensation insurance, or not complying with labor and licensing laws, complete an *Underground Economy Operations Lead Referral/Complaint Form* (DE 660 in English or DE 660/S in Spanish) (PDF) or contact the UEO at:

Hotline: 1-800-528-1783   **Email:** ueo@edd.ca.gov
Fax: 1-916-227-2772   **Online:** askedd.edd.ca.gov/ReportFraud.aspx

- To obtain the brochure *Paying Cash Wages "Under the Table"* (DE 573CA in English or DE 573CA/S in Spanish), visit Payroll Taxes - Forms and Publications (edd.ca.gov/payroll_taxes/forms_and_publications.htm) or order copies online at Forms and Publications (edd.ca.gov/forms).

- Further information about how to help the EDD fight fraud may be found in the brochure *Help Us Fight Fraud* (DE 2370) (PDF) (edd.ca.gov/pdf_pub_ctr/de2370.pdf).

What Are Wages?

Wages are all compensation for an employee's personal services, whether paid by check, cash, electronic debit, or the reasonable cash value of noncash payments, such as meals and lodging. The method of payment, whether by private agreement, consent, or mandate, does not change the taxability of wages paid to employees. Payments are considered wages even if the employee is a casual worker, a day or contract laborer, part-time or temporary worker, or paid by the day, hour, or any other method or measurement. Supplemental payments, including bonuses, overtime pay, sales awards, commissions, and vacation pay are also considered wages.

Subject Wages

Generally, all wages, unless excluded under the California Unemployment Insurance Code (CUIC), are considered subject wages and are used to determine the amount of Unemployment Insurance (UI), Employment Training Tax (ETT), Disability Insurance (DI), and Paid Family Leave (PFL) benefits a claimant should receive. Subject wages are the full amount of wages, regardless of the UI taxable wage limits. Refer to the inside front cover for UI taxable wage limits. Enter the Total Subject Wages in *Item F* for each employee on the *Quarterly Contribution Return and Report of Wages (Continuation)* (DE 9C). Certain types of employment and payments are not considered subject wages. Refer to *Information Sheet: Types of Employment* (DE 231TE) and *Information Sheet: Types of Payments* (DE 231TP) online at Forms and Publications (edd.ca.gov/payroll_taxes/forms_and_publications.htm) or contact the Taxpayer Assistance Center at 1-888-745-3886.

Personal Income Tax Wages

Personal Income Tax (PIT) wages are cash and noncash payments subject to state income tax and must be reported on an individual's California income tax return. Most payments for employees' services are reportable as PIT wages. An employee's PIT wage calendar year total should agree with the amount reported on the employee's federal *Wage and Tax Statement* (Form W-2) in Box 16 (state wages, tips, etc.). The PIT wages for each employee must be reported quarterly in Item G on the DE 9C. For additional information, refer to *Information Sheet: Personal Income Tax Wages Reported on the Quarterly Contribution Return and Report of Wages (Continuation) (DE 9C) (DE 231PIT) (PDF)* (edd.ca.gov/pdf_pub_ctr/de231pit.pdf) or contact the Taxpayer Assistance Center at 1-888-745-3886.

Note: Some wages excluded from PIT withholding are still considered PIT wages and must be reported to the EDD. For example, wages paid to agricultural workers.

Are Subject Wages and Personal Income Tax Wages the Same?

In most situations, when wages are subject to UI, ETT, SDI, and PIT withholding, subject wages and PIT wages are the same. Examples of when subject wages and PIT wages are different are:

- Employee salary reduction contributions to a qualified retirement or pension plan are generally included as subject wages, but are not reportable as PIT wages. Refer to the *Retirement and Pension Plans* section of *Information Sheet: Types of Payments (DE 231TP) (PDF)* (edd.ca.gov/pdf_pub_ctr/de231tp.pdf) or contact the Taxpayer Assistance Center at 1-888-745-3886.

- Under certain situations, wages paid to family employees (a child under the age of 18 years employed by own father or mother, an individual employed by own son, daughter, spouse, or registered domestic partner) may not be reported as subject wages but are reportable as PIT wages. Refer to the *Family Employees* section of *Information Sheet: Types of Employment (DE 231TE) (PDF)* (edd.ca.gov/pdf_pub_ctr/de231te.pdf) or contact the Taxpayer Assistance Center at 1-888-745-3886.

- Payments made to employees of churches are not reported as subject wages, but are reportable as PIT wages. Refer to the *Nonprofit Organization Employees* section of *Information Sheet: Types of Employment (DE 231TE)* (edd.ca.gov/pdf_pub_ctr/de231te.pdf) or contact the Taxpayer Assistance Center at 1-888-745-3886.

Employers Subject to California Personal Income Tax Only

Employers who are only required to withhold California PIT, but not the other payroll taxes, are still required to register with the EDD using the *Employers Depositing Only Personal Income Tax Withholding Registration and Update Form (DE 1P)* (edd.ca.gov/siteassets/files/pdf_pub_ctr/de1p.pdf). The employer is liable for the required PIT, whether or not it is withheld. By law, the filing of federal Form 1099-MISC or Form 1099-NEC, issued to the employee, with the Internal Revenue Service (IRS) or Franchise Tax Board (FTB) does not relieve the employer of liability.

Meals and Lodging

Meals and lodging provided free of charge or at a reduced rate to an employee are wages. If your employees are covered under a contract of employment or union agreement, the taxable value of meals and lodging cannot be less than the estimated value stated in the contract or agreement. Meals and lodging furnished for the employer's convenience and on the employer's premises are not subject to PIT.

If the cash value is not stated in an employment contract or union agreement, refer to the table below for the value of the meals and lodging. To determine the value of lodging, multiply the amount you could rent the property for (ordinary rental value) by 66 2/3 percent (0.6667). Ordinary rental value may be calculated on a monthly or weekly basis as follows:

	Value of Meals					Value of Lodging	
Year	Three Meals Per Day	Breakfast	Lunch	Dinner	Meal Not Identified	Minimum Per Week	Maximum Per Month
2024	$ 14.85	$ 3.05	$ 4.55	$ 7.25	$ 5.35	$ 60.05	$ 1,852
2023	$ 13.85	$ 2.85	$ 4.25	$ 6.75	$ 4.95	$ 57.05	$ 1,759

The values above apply to non-maritime employees only.

For more information on meals and lodging, including values for those provided to maritime employees, visit Payroll Taxes Rates and Withholding (edd.ca.gov/payroll_taxes/rates_and_withholding.htm) or contact the Taxpayer Assistance Center at 1-888-745-3886. If outside the U.S. or Canada, call 1-916-464-3502.

For historical rate information for the last eight years, visit the _Tax Rates, Wage Limits, and Value of Meals and Lodging (DE 3395) (PDF)_ (edd.ca.gov/pdf_pub_ctr/de3395.pdf).

Additional Information

- Who Is an Employee? Refer to page 8.
- EDD forms and publications (edd.ca.gov/payroll_taxes/forms_and_publications.htm)
- Information Sheets:
  - _Wages (DE 231A)_ (edd.ca.gov/siteassets/files/pdf_pub_ctr/de231a.pdf)
  - _Types of Employment (DE 231TE)_ (edd.ca.gov/siteassets/files/pdf_pub_ctr/de231te.pdf)
  - _Types of Payments (DE 231TP)_ (edd.ca.gov/siteassets/files/pdf_pub_ctr/de231tp.pdf)
  - _Personal Income Tax Wages Reported on the Quarterly Contribution Return and Report of Wages (Continuation) (DE 9C) (DE 231 PIT)_ (edd.ca.gov/siteassets/files/pdf_pub_ctr/de231pit.pdf)

For the latest tax news and employer resources,
visit California Employer News and Updates
(edd.ca.gov/payroll_taxes/employer-news.htm).

Subscribe to the EDD no-cost email subscription services
(edd.ca.gov/about_edd/get_email_notices.htm).

What Are Wages?

Personal Income Tax Wages Subject to California Withholding

With certain exceptions, compensation for services performed by an employee is considered wages and subject to Personal Income Tax (PIT) withholding. California wages include, but are not limited to, salaries, bonuses, commissions, fees (except fees paid to public officials), and payments in forms other than checks or cash. Wages in any form other than checks or cash are measured by the fair market value of the goods, lodging, meals, or other compensation given in payment for the employee's services.

How to Determine Which Wages Require PIT Withholding

Employers are required to withhold California PIT withholding on most wages. To determine which wages require PIT withholding, refer to *Information Sheet: Types of Employment* (DE 231TE) and *Information Sheet: Types of Payments* (DE 231TP). These information sheets identify special classes of employment and special types of payments and their treatment for Unemployment Insurance (UI), Employment Training Tax (ETT), State Disability Insurance (SDI), and California PIT wages and withholding. Also refer to *Classifying Employees* on page 8.

To obtain information sheets for specific industries and types of services, visit Forms and Publications (edd.ca.gov/payroll_taxes/forms_and_publications.htm) or contact the Taxpayer Assistance Center at 1-888-745-3886. If outside the U.S. or Canada, contact 1-916-464-3502.

Marital Status, Withholding Allowances, and Exemptions Form W-4 and DE 4

Beginning January 1, 2020, the IRS's *Employee's Withholding Certificate* (Form W-4) is used for federal income tax withholding only. The employee must file the state form *Employee's Withholding Allowance Certificate* (DE 4) for the appropriate PIT withholding.

If employees expect to itemize deductions on their California income tax return, they can claim additional withholding allowances, which are greater than their regular withholding allowances. When reduced withholding amounts are appropriate because of large amounts of itemized deductions, employees must complete a DE 4, including the attached worksheets, to support additional allowances for the itemized deductions. For information on treatment of additional withholding allowances for estimated deductions, refer to *Instructions for Additional Withholding Allowances for Estimated Deductions* on page 17 and the *Estimated Deduction* table on page 19.

Use of the DE 4 is no longer optional. When employees provide you with a DE 4, you must use it to determine their California PIT withholdings. You can download the DE 4 (PDF) (edd.ca.gov/pdf_pub_ctr/de4.pdf) or contact the Taxpayer Assistance Center at 1-888-745-3886.

Employees may request that no California PIT be withheld if they meet both of the following conditions:

- Incurred no liability for federal or state income tax for the prior tax year.

- Anticipate that no federal or state income tax liability will be incurred for the current tax year.

 Action Required: Each employee must complete a DE 4 with the word *Exempt* in Line 1. The exemption is good for one year.

If	Then
Employee does not file a DE 4	You may use the existing withholding certificate in your file to withhold. If you have no existing withholding certificate from the employee, then you must use Single with Zero withholding allowance. **Exception:** Do not withhold any California PIT from wages of employees who have filed *Exempt* on their DE 4 unless you receive a written notice from the FTB to withhold at a special rate. To maintain *Exempt* status, the employee **must** file a new DE 4 **each year** on or before February 15.
Employee files a DE 4	You **must** use the DE 4 to calculate and withhold California PIT.
Employee's marital status cannot be determined from the DE 4	Request the employee to correct the DE 4 or submit a new one. Until the new or corrected form is received, consider the employee as Single with Zero withholding allowances for California PIT withholding purposes.
Employee admits that DE 4 is false	When you receive an invalid DE 4, do not use it to calculate PIT withholding. Ask the employee for a new DE 4. If the employee does not give you a valid DE 4, withhold PIT as if the employee was single and claiming no withholding allowances. However, if you have an earlier Form W-4 or DE 4 for this employee that is valid, withhold as you did before.

Employer Obligations for Forms W-4 and DE 4

When you hire an employee, you must have the employee complete and provide a signed withholding exemption certificate, federal Form W-4 and a DE 4. The Form W-4 is used to withhold federal income tax and the DE 4 is used for the appropriate California Personal Income Tax (PIT) withholding. If an employee fails to give you a properly completed DE 4, you must withhold state income taxes from the employee's wages as if the employee were single and claiming no withholding allowances.

The requirements for a complete exemption from state wage withholding are the same as the federal requirements. You will not deduct and withhold any tax upon a payment of wages made to an employee if there is in effect, for the federal income tax purposes, with respect to the payment a withholding exemption certificate provided to the employer by the employee which contains statements that both:

- The employee incurred no liability for federal income tax imposed for the preceding tax year.

- The employee anticipates that they will incur no liability for federal income tax for the current tax year.

A DE 4 claiming exemption from withholding is valid only during the calendar year it was filed with the employer. To continue exemption from withholding in the next year, an employee must give you a new DE 4 claiming exempt status by February 15 of that year. If the employee does not give you a new DE 4, withhold tax as if the employee is single, with zero withholding allowances. However, if you have an earlier Form W-4 or DE 4 for this employee (not claiming exempt status) that is valid, withhold as you did before.

Employers must retain the federal Form W-4 and state DE 4 in their payroll records.

The DE 4 is considered invalid* if either of the following two conditions exist:

- The employee makes major changes to DE 4, such as crossing out words or writing more than is asked.

- The employee admits that the DE 4 is false.

When you receive an invalid DE 4, do not use it to calculate PIT withholding. Tell the employee that it is invalid and ask for another one. If the employee does not give you a valid form, withhold PIT as if the employee was single and claiming no withholding allowances. However, if you have an earlier Form W-4 or DE 4 for this employee that is valid, withhold as you did before.

FTB or the EDD may, by special direction in writing, require you, as the employer, to submit a Form W-4 or DE 4 when such forms are necessary for the administration of the withholding tax programs.

* Pursuant to Section 31.3402(f)(2)-1(e) of Title 26, Code of Federal Regulations, and Section 4340-1(b) of Title 22, California Code of Regulations.

Go Paperless!
You can view or download this guide at California Employer Guides
(edd.ca.gov/en/Payroll_Taxes/Employers_Guides).

Subscribe to the EDD no-cost email subscription services
(edd.ca.gov/about_edd/get_email_notices.htm).

California Personal
Income Tax Withholding

How to Determine PIT Withholding Amounts

Refer to page 17 for the 2024 PIT withholding schedules and information on how to calculate withholdings.

What if Your Employee Wants Additional PIT Withholding?

In addition to the tax withholding requirement from salaries and wages, you may, upon written request from the employee, agree to withhold an additional amount from the employee's wages. This agreement will be effective for the periods you and the employee mutually agree upon or until written termination of the agreement.

If employees rely on the Form W-4 instructions when calculating California withholding allowances, their California PIT could be significantly under withheld. This is particularly true if the household income is derived from more than one source. In order to determine the appropriate California PIT withholding, employees must complete the DE 4. If an employee wants more California PIT withheld than the schedules and the alternate methods allow, the employee should either request additional withholding or, if married, indicate *single* on the DE 4. For more information, refer to the DE 4 form and instructions.

How to Withhold PIT on Supplemental Wages

Supplemental wages include, but are not limited to, bonuses, overtime pay, sales awards, commissions, stock options, vacation pay, and dismissal or severance pay. Under certain circumstances, bonuses and stock options are taxed at a different flat rate than other types of supplemental wages. Refer to **Supplemental Wages** below. This only applies to stock options that are considered wages subject to PIT withholding.

If the supplemental wage is given to the employee at the same time as the employee's regular wages are paid, you are **required** to treat the sum of the payments as regular wages and withhold PIT based on the regular payroll period using the PIT withholding schedules.

If the supplemental wage is **not** given to the employee at the same time as the employee's regular wages are paid, you may use either of the following two options:

1. Compute the amount of PIT to withhold from the supplemental wage based on the combined regular wages and the supplemental wage. Compute the PIT withholding on the total of the supplemental wage and the current or most recent regular (gross) wage payment using the PIT withholding schedules. From that amount, subtract the PIT you withheld from the regular wages. The difference is the PIT amount you should withhold from the supplemental wages.

    or

2. Withhold the percentage noted below on the following types of supplemental wages without allowing for any withholding allowances claimed by the employee:

Supplemental Wages	Percentage
Bonuses and stock options	10.23 percent (.1023)
Other types (such as overtime pay, commissions, sales awards, severance, and vacation pay)	6.6 percent (.066)

To find out if stock options are wages subject to PIT withholding, obtain *Information Sheet: Stock Options* (DE 231SK) (PDF) (edd.ca.gov/pdf_pub_ctr/de231sk.pdf) or contact the Taxpayer Assistance Center at 1-888-745-3886.

Quarterly Estimated Payments

Wages are subject to mandatory California PIT withholding at the time they are paid to the employee. Quarterly estimates paid directly to the FTB are intended to satisfy taxes on income that is not subject to withholding. Quarterly estimates paid by an employee directly to FTB instead of proper withholdings from wages may result in an assessment to the employer. If you have questions regarding quarterly estimated payments, contact FTB at 1-800-852-5711.

Wages Paid to California Residents

If	Then
A California resident performs services in California or in another state.	Wages paid to the resident employee are subject to California PIT withholding, and PIT must be withheld from all wages paid, in accordance with the employee's DE 4. Refer to the withholding requirements on page 13. The wages paid must be reported as PIT wages on the *Quarterly Contribution Return and Report of Wages (Continuation)* (DE 9C). The PIT withheld must also be reported on the DE 9C.
A California resident performs services that are subject to personal income tax withholding laws of both California and another state, political subdivision, or the District of Columbia.	Make the withholding required by the other jurisdiction, and either: • For California, withhold the amount by which the California withholding amount exceeds the withholding amount for the other jurisdiction. • Do not withhold any California PIT if the withholding amount for the other jurisdiction is equal to, or greater than, the withholding amount for California. The wages reported as PIT wages on the *Quarterly Contribution Return and Report of Wages (Continuation)* (DE 9C) for the year should be the same wages that are entered in *Box 16* on your employee's Form W-2. The PIT withheld must also be reported on the DE 9C.

Wages Paid to Nonresidents of California

If	Then
A nonresident employee performs their entire service within California during the year (may include spouse of a military service member).	The wages paid to the nonresident employee are subject to California PIT withholding. The PIT must be withheld from all wages paid in accordance with the employee's DE 4. However, the spouse of a military service member may exclude wages from California PIT withholding by marking the corresponding box when filing a DE 4. Refer to the withholding requirements on page 13. The wages paid must be reported as PIT wages on the DE 9C. The PIT withheld must also be reported on the DE 9C.
A nonresident employee performs services both in California as well as in another state.	Only the wages earned in California are subject to California PIT withholding. The amount of wages subject to California PIT withholding is that portion of the total number of working days employed in California compared to the total number of working days employed in both California and the other state. The California wages must be reported as PIT wages on the DE 9C. The PIT withheld must also be reported on the DE 9C. **Note:** For employees whose compensation depends on the volume of business transacted, the amount of earnings subject to California PIT withholding is that portion received for the volume of business transacted in California compared to the total volume of business in both California and the other state.

PIT Withholding on Payments to Nonresident Independent Contractors

For more withholding information, refer to FTB Publication 1017 *Resident and Nonresident Withholding Guidelines* (ftb.ca.gov/forms/misc/1017.html) for guidance regarding PIT withholding on payments to nonresident independent contractors for services performed in California or contact FTB at 1-888-792-4900.

Additional Information

- EDD forms and publications (edd.ca.gov/payroll_taxes/forms_and_publications.htm):
- Information Sheets:
    - *Multistate Employment* (DE 231D)
    - *Withholding From Pensions, Annuities, and Certain Other Deferred Income* (DE 231P)
    - *Personal Income Tax Withholding – Supplemental Wage Payments, Moving Expense Reimbursement – WARN Act Payments* (DE 231PS)
    - *Third-Party Sick Pay* (DE 231R)
    - *Types of Employment* (DE 231TE)
    - *Types of Payments* (DE 231TP)

California Withholding Schedules for 2024

California provides two methods for determining the amount of wages and salaries to be withheld for state personal income tax:

- Method A – Wage Bracket Table Method **(Limited to wages or salaries less than $1 million)**
- Method B – Exact Calculation Method

   Method A provides a quick and easy way to select the appropriate withholding amount, based on the payroll period, filing status, and number of withholding allowances (regular and additional) if claimed. The *standard deduction* and *exemption allowance credit* are **already** included in the wage bracket tables. Even though this method involves fewer computations than Method B, it cannot be used with your computer in determining amounts to be withheld.

   Method B may be used to calculate withholding amounts either manually or by computer. This method will give an exact amount of tax to withhold. To use this method, you must enter the payroll period, filing status, number of withholding allowances, standard deduction, and exemption allowance credit amounts. These amounts are included in Tables 1 through 5 of the *Exact Calculation Section*.

If there are any questions concerning the operation or methodology of Method B for computer software, you may contact:

   Franchise Tax Board, Statistical Solutions and Modeling Section – 516, Mail Stop A-351
   PO Box 942840, Sacramento, CA 94240.

Special Note for Married Employees With Employed Spouses: To avoid underwithholding of state income tax liability we recommend that you use one of the following options: Single filing status to compute withholding amounts for the employee and spouse; **or** withhold an additional flat amount of tax.

Instructions for additional withholding allowances for estimated deductions:

All additional allowances for *Estimated Deductions* that are claimed on an *Employee's Withholding Allowance Certificate* (DE 4) must be used to reduce the amount of salaries and wages subject to withholding by using steps 1 and 2 shown below. If the *Employee's Withholding Allowance Certificate* (Form W-4) is used for California withholding purposes, all additional allowances for *Estimated Deductions* claimed must be treated as regular withholding allowances, **unless** the employee requests in writing that they be treated in accordance with the following:

1. Subtract the employee's estimated deduction allowance shown in the Table 2 - Estimated Deduction Table from the gross wages subject to withholding; and

2. Compute the tax to be withheld using:

   Method A – Wage Bracket Table Method
   Method B – Exact Calculation Method

If the DE 4 is used for California withholding purposes, compute the tax to be deducted and withheld based on the total number of regular withholding allowances claimed on line 1 of the DE 4.

If the Form W-4 is used for California withholding purposes, compute the tax to be deducted and withheld based on the total number of withholding allowances claimed on line 5 of Form W-4; minus the number of additional allowances for estimated deductions claimed. If Form W-4 does not separately identify the number of additional allowances for estimated deductions, the employee's request must specify the number claimed. The employee's request will remain in effect until the employee terminates it by furnishing a signed written notice or by furnishing a DE 4.

Employers may require employees to file a DE 4 when they wish to use additional allowances for estimated deductions to reduce the amount of wages subject to withholding.

As of January 1, 2020, the Form W-4 will be used for federal income tax withholding only. You must file a DE 4 to determine the appropriate California PIT withholding. If you do not provide your employer with a withholding certificate, the employer must use Single with Zero withholding allowance.

California Withholding Schedules for 2024

Method A – Wage Bracket Table Method

To determine the amount of tax to be withheld, follow these steps:

Step 1 Determine if the employee's gross wages are **less** than, or equal to, the amount shown in Table 1 – Low Income Exemption Table. If so, no income tax is required to be withheld.

Step 2 If the employee claims any additional withholding allowances for deductions, subtract the amount shown in Table 2 – Estimated Deduction Table from the gross wages.

Step 3 Subtract the number of additional withholding allowances from the total allowances to obtain the net allowances for tax computational purposes.

Step 4 Refer to the correct wage bracket table to arrive at the amount of tax to be withheld.

Example A: Method A – Wage Bracket Table Method. Weekly earnings of $900, married, and claiming five withholding allowances on Form W-4 or DE 4, three of which are for estimated deductions.

Step 1 Earnings for the weekly pay period of $900 are *greater* than the amount shown in Table 1 – Low Income Exemption Table ($683); therefore, income tax should be withheld.

Step 2
Earnings for the payroll period	$900.00
Subtract amount from Table 2 – Estimated Deduction Table	-58.00
Salaries and wages subject to withholding	$842.00

Step 3
Total number of withholding allowances claimed	5
Subtract number of estimated deduction allowances claimed	-3
Net allowances for tax computation purposes	2

Step 4 Refer to the appropriate wage bracket table weekly taxable earnings of $842 with two deductions to arrive at the amount of tax to be withheld. $3.67

Example B: Method A – Wage Bracket Table Method. Monthly earnings of $3,500, married, and claiming six withholding allowances on Form W-4 or DE 4, four of which are for estimated deductions.

Step 1 Earnings for the monthly payroll period are *greater* than the amount shown in Table 1 – Low Income Exemption Table ($2,962); therefore, income tax should be withheld.

Step 2
Earnings for the payroll period.	$3,500.00
Subtract amount from Table 2 – Estimated Deduction Table.	-333.00
Salaries and wages subject to withholding.	$3,167.00

Step 3
Total number of withholding allowances claimed.	6
Subtract number of estimated deduction allowances claimed.	-4
Net allowances for tax computation purposes.	2

Step 4 Refer to the appropriate wage bracket table (monthly taxable earnings of $3,167 with two deductions) to arrive at the amount of tax to be withheld. $5.02

California Withholding Schedules for 2024

METHOD A---WAGE BRACKET TABLE METHOD

TABLE 1 - LOW INCOME EXEMPTION TABLE

PAYROLL PERIOD	SINGLE, DUAL INCOME MARRIED OR MARRIED WITH MULTIPLE EMPLOYERS	MARRIED		UNMARRIED HEAD OF HOUSEHOLD
		ALLOWANCES ON DE 4 OR FORM W-4		
		'0' OR '1'	'2' OR MORE	
WEEKLY	$342	$342	$683	$683
BIWEEKLY	$683	$683	$1,367	$1,367
SEMI-MONTHLY	$740	$740	$1,481	$1,481
MONTHLY	$1,481	$1,481	$2,962	$2,962
QUARTERLY	$4,442	$4,442	$8,885	$8,885
SEMI-ANNUAL	$8,885	$8,885	$17,769	$17,769
ANNUAL	$17,769	$17,769	$35,538	$35,538
DAILY/MISCELLANEOUS	$68	$68	$137	$137

TABLE 2 - ESTIMATED DEDUCTION TABLE

ADDITIONAL WITHHOLDING ALLOWANCES *	PAYROLL PERIOD							
	WEEKLY	BI-WEEKLY	SEMI-MONTHLY	MONTHLY	QUARTERLY	SEMI-ANNUAL	ANNUAL	DAILY/MISC.
1	$19	$38	$42	$83	$250	$500	$1,000	$4
2	$38	$77	$83	$167	$500	$1,000	$2,000	$8
3	$58	$115	$125	$250	$750	$1,500	$3,000	$12
4	$77	$154	$167	$333	$1,000	$2,000	$4,000	$15
5	$96	$192	$208	$417	$1,250	$2,500	$5,000	$19
6	$115	$231	$250	$500	$1,500	$3,000	$6,000	$23
7	$135	$269	$292	$583	$1,750	$3,500	$7,000	$27
8	$154	$308	$333	$667	$2,000	$4,000	$8,000	$31
9	$173	$346	$375	$750	$2,250	$4,500	$9,000	$35
10**	$192	$385	$417	$833	$2,500	$5,000	$10,000	$38

*Number of Additional Withholding Allowances for Estimated Deductions claimed on Form W-4 or DE 4.

** If the number of Additional Withholding Allowances for Estimated Deductions claimed is greater than 10, multiply the amount shown for one Additional Allowance by the number claimed.

California Withholding Schedules for 2024

FOR WAGES PAID IN 2024

IF WAGES ARE...   AND THE NUMBER OF WITHHOLDING ALLOWANCES CLAIMED IS...

AT LEAST	BUT LESS THAN	0	1	2	3	4	5	6	7	8	9	10 OR MORE
		...THE AMOUNT OF INCOME TAX TO BE WITHHELD SHALL BE...										
$1	$160											
160	170	0.68										
170	180	0.79										
180	190	0.90										
190	200	1.01										
200	210	1.12										
210	220	1.23										
220	230	1.34										
230	240	1.45										
240	250	1.56										
250	260	1.67										
260	270	1.78										
270	280	1.89										
280	290	2.00										
290	300	2.11										
300	310	2.24										
310	320	2.46										
320	330	2.68										
330	340	2.90										
340	350	3.12	0.07									
350	360	3.34	0.29									
360	370	3.56	0.51									
370	380	3.78	0.73									
380	390	4.00	0.95									
390	400	4.22	1.17									
400	410	4.44	1.39									
410	420	4.66	1.61									
420	430	4.88	1.83									
430	440	5.10	2.05									
440	450	5.32	2.27									
450	460	5.54	2.49									
460	480	5.87	2.82									
480	500	6.31	3.26	0.22								
500	520	6.75	3.70	0.66								
520	540	7.19	4.14	1.10								
540	560	7.63	4.58	1.54								
560	600	8.33	5.29	2.24								
600	640	10.09	7.05	4.00	0.95							
640	680	11.85	8.81	5.76	2.71							
680	720	13.61	10.57	7.52	4.47	1.42						
720	760	15.37	12.33	9.28	6.23	3.18	0.14					
760	800	17.13	14.09	11.04	7.99	4.94	1.90					
800	840	18.89	15.85	12.80	9.75	6.70	3.66	0.61				
840	880	20.83	17.78	14.73	11.68	8.64	5.59	2.54				
880	920	23.47	20.42	17.37	14.32	11.28	8.23	5.18	2.14			
920	970	26.44	23.39	20.34	17.29	14.25	11.20	8.15	5.11	2.06		
970	1070	31.39	28.34	25.29	22.24	19.20	16.15	13.10	10.06	7.01	3.96	0.92
1070	1180	38.32	35.27	32.22	29.17	26.13	23.08	20.03	16.99	13.94	10.89	7.85
1180	1290	47.60	44.55	41.50	38.46	35.41	32.36	29.31	26.27	23.22	20.17	17.13
1290	1400	57.28	54.23	51.18	48.14	45.09	42.04	38.99	35.95	32.90	29.85	26.81
1400	1510	67.50	64.45	61.40	58.36	55.31	52.26	49.22	46.17	43.12	40.08	37.03

1510 and over   (Use Method B - Exact Calculation Method)

California Withholding Schedules For 2024

California Withholding Schedules for 2024

MARRIED PERSONS----WEEKLY PAYROLL PERIOD

FOR WAGES PAID IN 2024

IF WAGES ARE...   AND THE NUMBER OF WITHHOLDING ALLOWANCES CLAIMED IS...

AT LEAST	BUT LESS THAN	0	1	2	3	4	5	6	7	8	9	10 OR MORE
		...THE AMOUNT OF INCOME TAX TO BE WITHHELD SHALL BE...										
$1	$160											
160	170	0.68										
170	180	0.79										
180	190	0.90										
190	200	1.01										
200	210	1.12										
210	220	1.23										
220	230	1.34										
230	240	1.45										
240	250	1.56										
250	260	1.67										
260	270	1.78										
270	280	1.89										
280	290	2.00										
290	300	2.11										
300	310	2.22										
310	320	2.33										
320	330	2.44										
330	340	2.55										
340	350	2.66										
350	360	2.77										
360	370	2.88										
370	380	2.99										
380	390	3.10	0.05									
390	400	3.21	0.16									
400	410	3.32	0.27									
410	420	3.43	0.38									
420	430	3.54	0.49									
430	440	3.65	0.60									
440	460	3.82	0.77									
460	480	4.04	0.99									
480	500	4.26	1.21									
500	520	4.55	1.50									
520	540	4.99	1.94									
540	560	5.43	2.38									
560	580	5.87	2.82									
580	600	6.31	3.26									
600	620	6.75	3.70									
620	640	7.19	4.14									
640	660	7.63	4.58									
660	680	8.07	5.02									
680	700	8.51	5.46	0.15								
700	720	8.95	5.90	0.59								
720	740	9.39	6.34	1.03								
740	760	9.83	6.78	1.47								
760	780	10.27	7.22	1.91								
780	800	10.71	7.66	2.35								
800	820	11.15	8.10	2.79								
820	840	11.59	8.54	3.23	0.18							
840	860	12.03	8.98	3.67	0.62							
860	880	12.47	9.42	4.11	1.06							

--- CONTINUED NEXT PAGE ---

California Withholding Schedules for 2024

MARRIED PERSONS----WEEKLY PAYROLL PERIOD

FOR WAGES PAID IN 2024

IF WAGES ARE...   AND THE NUMBER OF WITHHOLDING ALLOWANCES CLAIMED IS...

AT LEAST	BUT LESS THAN	0	1	2	3	4	5	6	7	8	9	10 OR MORE
		...THE AMOUNT OF INCOME TAX TO BE WITHHELD SHALL BE...										
880	900	12.91	9.86	4.55	1.50							
900	920	13.35	10.30	4.99	1.94							
920	940	13.79	10.74	5.43	2.38							
940	960	14.23	11.18	5.87	2.82							
960	980	14.67	11.62	6.31	3.26	0.21						
980	1000	15.11	12.06	6.75	3.70	0.65						
1000	1020	15.55	12.50	7.19	4.14	1.09						
1020	1040	15.99	12.94	7.63	4.58	1.53						
1040	1060	16.43	13.38	8.07	5.02	1.97						
1060	1080	17.24	14.20	8.51	5.46	2.41						
1080	1100	18.12	15.08	8.95	5.90	2.85						
1100	1120	19.00	15.96	9.39	6.34	3.29	0.25					
1120	1140	19.88	16.84	9.83	6.78	3.73	0.69					
1140	1170	20.98	17.94	10.38	7.33	4.28	1.24					
1170	1200	22.30	19.26	11.67	8.62	5.58	2.53					
1200	1230	23.62	20.58	12.99	9.94	6.90	3.85	0.80				
1230	1260	24.94	21.90	14.31	11.26	8.22	5.17	2.12				
1260	1290	26.26	23.22	15.63	12.58	9.54	6.49	3.44	0.40			
1290	1320	27.58	24.54	16.95	13.90	10.86	7.81	4.76	1.72			
1320	1350	28.90	25.86	18.27	15.22	12.18	9.13	6.08	3.04			
1350	1390	30.44	27.40	19.81	16.76	13.72	10.67	7.62	4.58	1.53		
1390	1430	32.20	29.16	21.57	18.52	15.48	12.43	9.38	6.34	3.29	0.24	
1430	1470	33.96	30.92	23.33	20.28	17.24	14.19	11.14	8.10	5.05	2.00	
1470	1510	35.72	32.68	25.09	22.04	19.00	15.95	12.90	9.86	6.81	3.76	0.71
1510	1550	37.48	34.44	26.85	23.80	20.76	17.71	14.66	11.62	8.57	5.52	2.47
1550	1590	39.24	36.20	28.61	25.56	22.52	19.47	16.42	13.38	10.33	7.28	4.23
1590	1630	41.20	38.15	30.37	27.32	24.28	21.23	18.18	15.14	12.09	9.04	5.99
1630	1670	43.84	40.79	32.13	29.08	26.04	22.99	19.94	16.90	13.85	10.80	7.75
1670	1710	46.48	43.43	33.89	30.84	27.80	24.75	21.70	18.66	15.61	12.56	9.51
1710	1750	49.12	46.07	36.22	33.17	30.12	27.08	24.03	20.98	17.93	14.89	11.84
1750	1810	52.42	49.37	39.52	36.47	33.42	30.38	27.33	24.28	21.23	18.19	15.14
1810	1870	56.38	53.33	43.48	40.43	37.38	34.34	31.29	28.24	25.19	22.15	19.10
1870	1950	61.00	57.95	48.10	45.05	42.00	38.96	35.91	32.86	29.81	26.77	23.72
1950	2030	66.28	63.23	53.38	50.33	47.28	44.24	41.19	38.14	35.09	32.05	29.00
2030	2130	72.22	69.17	59.32	56.27	53.22	50.18	47.13	44.08	41.03	37.99	34.94
2130	2300	81.83	78.78	68.23	65.18	62.13	59.09	56.04	52.99	49.94	46.90	43.85
2300	2470	96.79	93.74	81.62	78.57	75.53	72.48	69.43	66.38	63.34	60.29	57.24
2470	2640	111.75	108.70	96.58	93.53	90.49	87.44	84.39	81.34	78.30	75.25	72.20
2640	2810	126.71	123.66	111.54	108.49	105.45	102.40	99.35	96.30	93.26	90.21	87.16
2810	2980	144.01	140.96	127.37	124.32	121.27	118.23	115.18	112.13	109.09	106.04	102.99

2980 and over   (Use Method B - Exact Calculation Method)

California Withholding Schedules for 2024

UNMARRIED HEAD OF HOUSEHOLD----WEEKLY PAYROLL PERIOD

FOR WAGES PAID IN 2024

IF WAGES ARE...   AND THE NUMBER OF WITHHOLDING ALLOWANCES CLAIMED IS...

AT LEAST	BUT LESS THAN	0	1	2	3	4	5	6	7	8	9	10 OR MORE
					...THE AMOUNT OF INCOME TAX TO BE WITHHELD SHALL BE...							
$1	$250											
250	260	0.54										
260	270	0.65										
270	280	0.76										
280	290	0.87										
290	300	0.98										
300	310	1.09										
310	320	1.20										
320	330	1.31										
330	340	1.42										
340	350	1.53										
350	360	1.64										
360	370	1.75										
370	380	1.86										
380	390	1.97										
390	400	2.08										
400	410	2.19										
410	420	2.30										
420	430	2.41										
430	440	2.52										
440	450	2.63										
450	460	2.74										
460	470	2.85										
470	480	2.96										
480	490	3.07	0.02									
490	500	3.18	0.13									
500	520	3.34	0.29									
520	540	3.56	0.51									
540	560	3.78	0.73									
560	580	4.00	0.95									
580	600	4.22	1.17									
600	620	4.47	1.42									
620	640	4.91	1.86									
640	660	5.35	2.30									
660	680	5.79	2.74									
680	700	6.23	3.18	0.14								
700	740	6.89	3.84	0.80								
740	780	7.77	4.72	1.68								
780	820	8.65	5.60	2.56								
820	860	9.53	6.48	3.44	0.39							
860	900	10.41	7.36	4.32	1.27							
900	950	11.40	8.35	5.31	2.26							
950	1010	12.61	9.56	6.52	3.47	0.42						
1010	1070	13.93	10.88	7.84	4.79	1.74						
1070	1150	15.47	12.42	9.38	6.33	3.28	0.24					
1150	1240	18.22	15.17	12.12	9.07	6.03	2.98					
1240	1370	23.06	20.01	16.96	13.91	10.87	7.82	4.77	1.73			
1370	1510	29.21	26.16	23.12	20.07	17.02	13.97	10.93	7.88	4.83	1.79	
1510	1660	38.78	35.73	32.69	29.64	26.59	23.54	20.50	17.45	14.40	11.36	8.31
1660	1810	48.98	45.94	42.89	39.84	36.79	33.75	30.70	27.65	24.61	21.56	18.51
1810	1970	62.62	59.58	56.53	53.48	50.43	47.39	44.34	41.29	38.25	35.20	32.15
1970	2130	77.48	74.44	71.39	68.34	65.30	62.25	59.20	56.16	53.11	50.06	47.01
2130	and over				(Use Method B - Exact Calculation Method)							

California Withholding Schedules For 2024

California Withholding Schedules for 2024

SINGLE PERSONS, DUAL INCOME MARRIED
OR MARRIED WITH MULTIPLE EMPLOYERS----BIWEEKLY PAYROLL PERIOD

FOR WAGES PAID IN 2024

IF WAGES ARE...   AND THE NUMBER OF WITHHOLDING ALLOWANCES CLAIMED IS...

AT LEAST	BUT LESS THAN	0	1	2	3	4	5	6	7	8	9	10 OR MORE
		...THE AMOUNT OF INCOME TAX TO BE WITHHELD SHALL BE...										
$1	$260											
260	280	0.70										
280	300	0.92										
300	320	1.14										
320	340	1.36										
340	360	1.58										
360	380	1.80										
380	400	2.02										
400	420	2.24										
420	440	2.46										
440	460	2.68										
460	480	2.90										
480	500	3.12										
500	520	3.34										
520	540	3.56										
540	560	3.78										
560	580	4.00										
580	600	4.22										
600	620	4.48										
620	640	4.92										
640	660	5.36										
660	680	5.80										
680	700	6.24	0.15									
700	720	6.68	0.59									
720	740	7.12	1.03									
740	760	7.56	1.47									
760	780	8.00	1.91									
780	800	8.44	2.35									
800	820	8.88	2.79									
820	860	9.54	3.45									
860	900	10.42	4.33									
900	940	11.30	5.21									
940	980	12.18	6.09									
980	1020	13.06	6.97	0.87								
1020	1070	14.05	7.96	1.86								
1070	1120	15.15	9.06	2.96								
1120	1170	16.25	10.16	4.06								
1170	1220	18.20	12.11	6.02								
1220	1270	20.40	14.31	8.22	2.12							
1270	1320	22.60	16.51	10.42	4.32							
1320	1370	24.80	18.71	12.62	6.52	0.43						
1370	1420	27.00	20.91	14.82	8.72	2.63						
1420	1470	29.20	23.11	17.02	10.92	4.83						
1470	1520	31.40	25.31	19.22	13.12	7.03	0.93					
1520	1620	34.70	28.61	22.52	16.42	10.33	4.23					
1620	1720	39.10	33.01	26.92	20.82	14.73	8.63	2.54				
1720	1920	48.25	42.16	36.06	29.97	23.87	17.78	11.69	5.59			
1920	2120	61.45	55.36	49.26	43.17	37.07	30.98	24.89	18.79	12.70	6.60	0.51
2120	2320	74.65	68.56	62.46	56.37	50.27	44.18	38.09	31.99	25.90	19.80	13.71
2320	2550	92.11	86.02	79.93	73.83	67.74	61.64	55.55	49.46	43.36	37.27	31.17
2550	2780	112.35	106.26	100.17	94.07	87.98	81.88	75.79	69.70	63.60	57.51	51.41
2780	3010	133.46	127.37	121.27	115.18	109.09	102.99	96.90	90.80	84.71	78.62	72.52

3010 and over   (Use Method B - Exact Calculation Method)

California Withholding Schedules for 2024

MARRIED PERSONS----BIWEEKLY PAYROLL PERIOD

FOR WAGES PAID IN 2024

IF WAGES ARE...   AND THE NUMBER OF WITHHOLDING ALLOWANCES CLAIMED IS...

AT LEAST	BUT LESS THAN	0	1	2	3	4	5	6	7	8	9	10 OR MORE
		...THE AMOUNT OF INCOME TAX TO BE WITHHELD SHALL BE...										
$1	$260											
260	280	0.70										
280	300	0.92										
300	320	1.14										
320	340	1.36										
340	360	1.58										
360	380	1.80										
380	400	2.02										
400	420	2.24										
420	440	2.46										
440	460	2.68										
460	480	2.90										
480	500	3.12										
500	520	3.34										
520	540	3.56										
540	560	3.78										
560	580	4.00										
580	600	4.22										
600	620	4.44										
620	640	4.66										
640	660	4.88										
660	680	5.10										
680	700	5.32										
700	720	5.54										
720	740	5.76										
740	760	5.98										
760	780	6.20	0.11									
780	800	6.42	0.33									
800	820	6.64	0.55									
820	840	6.86	0.77									
840	860	7.08	0.99									
860	880	7.30	1.21									
880	900	7.52	1.43									
900	920	7.74	1.65									
920	940	7.96	1.87									
940	960	8.18	2.09									
960	980	8.40	2.31									
980	1000	8.62	2.53									
1000	1020	8.88	2.79									
1020	1060	9.54	3.45									
1060	1100	10.42	4.33									
1100	1140	11.30	5.21									
1140	1180	12.18	6.09									
1180	1220	13.06	6.97	0.87								
1220	1260	13.94	7.85	1.75								
1260	1300	14.82	8.73	2.63								
1300	1340	15.70	9.61	3.51								
1340	1380	16.58	10.49	4.39								
1380	1420	17.46	11.37	5.27								
1420	1460	18.34	12.25	6.15	0.06							
1460	1500	19.22	13.13	7.03	0.94							

--- CONTINUED NEXT PAGE ---

California Withholding Schedules For 2024

California Withholding Schedules for 2024

MARRIED PERSONS----BIWEEKLY PAYROLL PERIOD

FOR WAGES PAID IN 2024

IF WAGES ARE...   AND THE NUMBER OF WITHHOLDING ALLOWANCES CLAIMED IS...

AT LEAST	BUT LESS THAN	0	1	2	3	4	5	6	7	8	9	10 OR MORE
1500	1540	20.10	14.01	7.91	1.82							
1540	1580	20.98	14.89	8.79	2.70							
1580	1620	21.86	15.77	9.67	3.58							
1620	1660	22.74	16.65	10.55	4.46							
1660	1700	23.62	17.53	11.43	5.34							
1700	1740	24.50	18.41	12.31	6.22	0.13						
1740	1780	25.38	19.29	13.19	7.10	1.01						
1780	1820	26.26	20.17	14.07	7.98	1.89						
1820	1860	27.14	21.05	14.95	8.86	2.77						
1860	1900	28.02	21.93	15.83	9.74	3.65						
1900	1940	28.90	22.81	16.71	10.62	4.53						
1940	1980	29.78	23.69	17.59	11.50	5.41						
1980	2020	30.66	24.57	18.47	12.38	6.29	0.19					
2020	2060	31.54	25.45	19.35	13.26	7.17	1.07					
2060	2100	32.42	26.33	20.23	14.14	8.05	1.95					
2100	2140	33.60	27.51	21.42	15.32	9.23	3.13					
2140	2180	35.36	29.27	23.18	17.08	10.99	4.89					
2180	2220	37.12	31.03	24.94	18.84	12.75	6.65	0.56				
2220	2260	38.88	32.79	26.70	20.60	14.51	8.41	2.32				
2260	2300	40.64	34.55	28.46	22.36	16.27	10.17	4.08				
2300	2350	42.62	36.53	30.44	24.34	18.25	12.15	6.06				
2350	2400	44.82	38.73	32.64	26.54	20.45	14.35	8.26	2.17			
2400	2450	47.02	40.93	34.84	28.74	22.65	16.55	10.46	4.37			
2450	2500	49.22	43.13	37.04	30.94	24.85	18.75	12.66	6.57	0.47		
2500	2550	51.42	45.33	39.24	33.14	27.05	20.95	14.86	8.77	2.67		
2550	2600	53.62	47.53	41.44	35.34	29.25	23.15	17.06	10.97	4.87		
2600	2650	55.82	49.73	43.64	37.54	31.45	25.35	19.26	13.17	7.07	0.98	
2650	2700	58.02	51.93	45.84	39.74	33.65	27.55	21.46	15.37	9.27	3.18	
2700	2750	60.22	54.13	48.04	41.94	35.85	29.75	23.66	17.57	11.47	5.38	
2750	2800	62.42	56.33	50.24	44.14	38.05	31.95	25.86	19.77	13.67	7.58	1.48
2800	2850	64.62	58.53	52.44	46.34	40.25	34.15	28.06	21.97	15.87	9.78	3.68
2850	2900	66.82	60.73	54.64	48.54	42.45	36.35	30.26	24.17	18.07	11.98	5.88
2900	2950	69.02	62.93	56.84	50.74	44.65	38.55	32.46	26.37	20.27	14.18	8.08
2950	3000	71.22	65.13	59.04	52.94	46.85	40.75	34.66	28.57	22.47	16.38	10.28
3000	3050	73.42	67.33	61.24	55.14	49.05	42.95	36.86	30.77	24.67	18.58	12.48
3050	3150	76.72	70.63	64.54	58.44	52.35	46.25	40.16	34.07	27.97	21.88	15.78
3150	3250	81.12	75.03	68.94	62.84	56.75	50.65	44.56	38.47	32.37	26.28	20.18
3250	3350	87.67	81.58	75.49	69.39	63.30	57.20	51.11	45.02	38.92	32.83	26.73
3350	3450	94.27	88.18	82.09	75.99	69.90	63.80	57.71	51.62	45.52	39.43	33.33
3450	3550	100.87	94.78	88.69	82.59	76.50	70.40	64.31	58.22	52.12	46.03	39.93
3550	3700	109.12	103.03	96.94	90.84	84.75	78.65	72.56	66.47	60.37	54.28	48.18
3700	3850	119.02	112.93	106.84	100.74	94.65	88.55	82.46	76.37	70.27	64.18	58.08
3850	4080	131.56	125.47	119.38	113.28	107.19	101.09	95.00	88.91	82.81	76.72	70.62
4080	4310	146.74	140.65	134.56	128.46	122.37	116.27	110.18	104.09	97.99	91.90	85.80
4310	4540	163.22	157.12	151.03	144.94	138.84	132.75	126.65	120.56	114.47	108.37	102.28
4540	4820	185.66	179.56	173.47	167.38	161.28	155.19	149.09	143.00	136.91	130.81	124.72
4820	5100	210.30	204.20	198.11	192.02	185.92	179.83	173.73	167.64	161.55	155.45	149.36
5100	5420	236.70	230.60	224.51	218.42	212.32	206.23	200.13	194.04	187.95	181.85	175.76
5420	5740	266.54	260.45	254.35	248.26	242.16	236.07	229.98	223.88	217.79	211.69	205.60

5740 and over   (Use Method B - Exact Calculation Method)

California Withholding Schedules For 2024

California Withholding Schedules for 2024

UNMARRIED HEAD OF HOUSEHOLD----BIWEEKLY PAYROLL PERIOD

FOR WAGES PAID IN 2024

IF WAGES ARE...   AND THE NUMBER OF WITHHOLDING ALLOWANCES CLAIMED IS...

AT LEAST	BUT LESS THAN	0	1	2	3	4	5	6	7	8	9	10 OR MORE
						...THE AMOUNT OF INCOME TAX TO BE WITHHELD SHALL BE...						
$1	$560											
560	580	1.73										
580	600	1.95										
600	620	2.17										
620	640	2.39										
640	660	2.61										
660	680	2.83										
680	700	3.05										
700	720	3.27										
720	740	3.49										
740	760	3.71										
760	780	3.93										
780	800	4.15										
800	820	4.37										
820	840	4.59										
840	860	4.81										
860	880	5.03										
880	900	5.25										
900	920	5.47										
920	940	5.69										
940	960	5.91										
960	980	6.13	0.04									
980	1000	6.35	0.26									
1000	1040	6.68	0.59									
1040	1080	7.12	1.03									
1080	1120	7.56	1.47									
1120	1160	8.00	1.91									
1160	1200	8.44	2.35									
1200	1250	9.05	2.96									
1250	1300	10.15	4.06									
1300	1350	11.25	5.16									
1350	1400	12.35	6.26	0.16								
1400	1450	13.45	7.36	1.26								
1450	1500	14.55	8.46	2.36								
1500	1550	15.65	9.56	3.46								
1550	1600	16.75	10.66	4.56								
1600	1650	17.85	11.76	5.66								
1650	1700	18.95	12.86	6.76	0.67							
1700	1750	20.05	13.96	7.86	1.77							
1750	1800	21.15	15.06	8.96	2.87							
1800	1850	22.25	16.16	10.06	3.97							
1850	1950	23.90	17.81	11.71	5.62							
1950	2050	26.10	20.01	13.91	7.82	1.73						
2050	2150	28.30	22.21	16.11	10.02	3.93						
2150	2250	30.50	24.41	18.31	12.22	6.13	0.03					
2250	2350	32.70	26.61	20.51	14.42	8.33	2.23					
2350	2500	37.97	31.88	25.78	19.69	13.60	7.50	1.41				
2500	2650	44.57	38.48	32.38	26.29	20.20	14.10	8.01	1.91			
2650	2850	52.27	46.18	40.08	33.99	27.90	21.80	15.71	9.61	3.52		
2850	3050	63.04	56.95	50.85	44.76	38.66	32.57	26.48	20.38	14.29	8.19	2.10
3050	3300	77.89	71.80	65.70	59.61	53.51	47.42	41.33	35.23	29.14	23.04	16.95
3300	3620	97.08	90.99	84.90	78.80	72.71	66.61	60.52	54.43	48.33	42.24	36.14
3620	3940	125.24	119.15	113.06	106.96	100.87	94.77	88.68	82.59	76.49	70.40	64.30
3940	4260	154.97	148.88	142.78	136.69	130.59	124.50	118.41	112.31	106.22	100.12	94.03

4260 and over   (Use Method B - Exact Calculation Method)

California Withholding Schedules For 2024

California Withholding Schedules for 2024

SINGLE PERSONS, DUAL INCOME MARRIED
OR MARRIED WITH MULTIPLE EMPLOYERS----SEMI-MONTHLY PAYROLL PERIOD

FOR WAGES PAID IN 2024

IF WAGES ARE...   AND THE NUMBER OF WITHHOLDING ALLOWANCES CLAIMED IS...

AT LEAST	BUT LESS THAN	0	1	2	3	4	5	6	7	8	9	10 OR MORE
							...THE AMOUNT OF INCOME TAX TO BE WITHHELD SHALL BE...					
$1	$300											
300	320	0.95										
320	340	1.17										
340	360	1.39										
360	380	1.61										
380	400	1.83										
400	420	2.05										
420	440	2.27										
440	460	2.49										
460	480	2.71										
480	500	2.93										
500	540	3.26										
540	580	3.70										
580	620	4.14										
620	660	4.58										
660	700	5.27										
700	740	6.15										
740	780	7.03	0.43									
780	820	7.91	1.31									
820	860	8.79	2.19									
860	900	9.67	3.07									
900	940	10.55	3.95									
940	980	11.43	4.83									
980	1020	12.31	5.71									
1020	1060	13.19	6.59									
1060	1100	14.07	7.47	0.87								
1100	1140	14.95	8.35	1.75								
1140	1180	15.83	9.23	2.63								
1180	1220	16.71	10.11	3.51								
1220	1260	17.59	10.99	4.39								
1260	1300	19.08	12.48	5.88								
1300	1340	20.84	14.24	7.64	1.04							
1340	1380	22.60	16.00	9.40	2.80							
1380	1420	24.36	17.76	11.16	4.56							
1420	1460	26.12	19.52	12.92	6.32							
1460	1500	27.88	21.28	14.68	8.08	1.48						
1500	1540	29.64	23.04	16.44	9.84	3.24						
1540	1580	31.40	24.80	18.20	11.60	5.00						
1580	1620	33.16	26.56	19.96	13.36	6.76	0.16					
1620	1660	34.92	28.32	21.72	15.12	8.52	1.92					
1660	1700	36.68	30.08	23.48	16.88	10.28	3.68					
1700	1750	38.66	32.06	25.46	18.86	12.26	5.66					
1750	1800	40.86	34.26	27.66	21.06	14.46	7.86	1.26				
1800	1850	43.06	36.46	29.86	23.26	16.66	10.06	3.46				
1850	2000	49.18	42.58	35.98	29.38	22.78	16.18	9.58	2.98			
2000	2150	59.08	52.48	45.88	39.28	32.68	26.08	19.48	12.88	6.28		
2150	2350	70.63	64.03	57.43	50.83	44.23	37.63	31.03	24.43	17.83	11.23	4.63
2350	2550	83.83	77.23	70.63	64.03	57.43	50.83	44.23	37.63	31.03	24.43	17.83
2550	2800	103.05	96.45	89.85	83.25	76.65	70.05	63.45	56.85	50.25	43.65	37.05
2800	3050	125.05	118.45	111.85	105.25	98.65	92.05	85.45	78.85	72.25	65.65	59.05
3050	3300	148.53	141.93	135.33	128.73	122.13	115.53	108.93	102.33	95.73	89.13	82.53

3300 and over   (Use Method B - Exact Calculation Method)

California Withholding Schedules For 2024

California Withholding Schedules for 2024

MARRIED PERSONS----SEMI-MONTHLY PAYROLL PERIOD

FOR WAGES PAID IN 2024

IF WAGES ARE...   AND THE NUMBER OF WITHHOLDING ALLOWANCES CLAIMED IS...

AT LEAST	BUT LESS THAN	0	1	2	3	4	5	6	7	8	9	10 OR MORE
					...THE AMOUNT OF INCOME TAX TO BE WITHHELD SHALL BE...							
$1	$300											
300	320	0.95										
320	340	1.17										
340	360	1.39										
360	380	1.61										
380	400	1.83										
400	420	2.05										
420	440	2.27										
440	460	2.49										
460	480	2.71										
480	500	2.93										
500	520	3.15										
520	540	3.37										
540	560	3.59										
560	580	3.81										
580	600	4.03										
600	620	4.25										
620	640	4.47										
640	660	4.69										
660	680	4.91										
680	700	5.13										
700	720	5.35										
720	740	5.57										
740	760	5.79										
760	780	6.01										
780	800	6.23										
800	820	6.45										
820	840	6.67	0.07									
840	860	6.89	0.29									
860	880	7.11	0.51									
880	900	7.33	0.73									
900	920	7.55	0.95									
920	940	7.77	1.17									
940	960	7.99	1.39									
960	980	8.21	1.61									
980	1000	8.43	1.83									
1000	1040	8.76	2.16									
1040	1080	9.20	2.60									
1080	1120	9.74	3.14									
1120	1160	10.62	4.02									
1160	1200	11.50	4.90									
1200	1240	12.38	5.78									
1240	1280	13.26	6.66									
1280	1320	14.14	7.54									
1320	1360	15.02	8.42									
1360	1400	15.90	9.30									
1400	1440	16.78	10.18									
1440	1480	17.66	11.06									
1480	1520	18.54	11.94	0.42								
1520	1560	19.42	12.82	1.30								
1560	1600	20.30	13.70	2.18								

--- CONTINUED NEXT PAGE ---

California Withholding Schedules For 2024

California Withholding Schedules for 2024

MARRIED PERSONS----SEMI-MONTHLY PAYROLL PERIOD

FOR WAGES PAID IN 2024

IF WAGES ARE...   AND THE NUMBER OF WITHHOLDING ALLOWANCES CLAIMED IS...

AT LEAST	BUT LESS THAN	0	1	2	3	4	5	6	7	8	9	10 OR MORE
		...THE AMOUNT OF INCOME TAX TO BE WITHHELD SHALL BE...										
1600	1640	21.18	14.58	3.06								
1640	1680	22.06	15.46	3.94								
1680	1720	22.94	16.34	4.82								
1720	1760	23.82	17.22	5.70								
1760	1800	24.70	18.10	6.58								
1800	1840	25.58	18.98	7.46	0.86							
1840	1880	26.46	19.86	8.34	1.74							
1880	1920	27.34	20.74	9.22	2.62							
1920	1960	28.22	21.62	10.10	3.50							
1960	2000	29.10	22.50	10.98	4.38							
2000	2040	29.98	23.38	11.86	5.26							
2040	2080	30.86	24.26	12.74	6.14							
2080	2120	31.74	25.14	13.62	7.02	0.42						
2120	2160	32.62	26.02	14.50	7.90	1.30						
2160	2200	33.50	26.90	15.38	8.78	2.18						
2200	2250	34.49	27.89	16.37	9.77	3.17						
2250	2300	35.59	28.99	17.47	10.87	4.27						
2300	2350	37.64	31.04	18.57	11.97	5.37						
2350	2400	39.84	33.24	19.67	13.07	6.47						
2400	2450	42.04	35.44	20.77	14.17	7.57	0.97					
2450	2500	44.24	37.64	21.87	15.27	8.67	2.07					
2500	2550	46.44	39.84	23.41	16.81	10.21	3.61					
2550	2600	48.64	42.04	25.61	19.01	12.41	5.81					
2600	2650	50.84	44.24	27.81	21.21	14.61	8.01	1.41				
2650	2700	53.04	46.44	30.01	23.41	16.81	10.21	3.61				
2700	2750	55.24	48.64	32.21	25.61	19.01	12.41	5.81				
2750	2800	57.44	50.84	34.41	27.81	21.21	14.61	8.01	1.41			
2800	2850	59.64	53.04	36.61	30.01	23.41	16.81	10.21	3.61			
2850	2900	61.84	55.24	38.81	32.21	25.61	19.01	12.41	5.81			
2900	2950	64.04	57.44	41.01	34.41	27.81	21.21	14.61	8.01	1.41		
2950	3000	66.24	59.64	43.21	36.61	30.01	23.41	16.81	10.21	3.61		
3000	3075	68.99	62.39	45.96	39.36	32.76	26.16	19.56	12.96	6.36		
3075	3150	72.29	65.69	49.26	42.66	36.06	29.46	22.86	16.26	9.66	3.06	
3150	3225	75.59	68.99	52.56	45.96	39.36	32.76	26.16	19.56	12.96	6.36	
3225	3300	78.89	72.29	55.86	49.26	42.66	36.06	29.46	22.86	16.26	9.66	3.06
3300	3375	82.19	75.59	59.16	52.56	45.96	39.36	32.76	26.16	19.56	12.96	6.36
3375	3475	86.04	79.44	63.01	56.41	49.81	43.21	36.61	30.01	23.41	16.81	10.21
3475	3575	91.67	85.07	67.41	60.81	54.21	47.61	41.01	34.41	27.81	21.21	14.61
3575	3675	98.27	91.67	71.81	65.21	58.61	52.01	45.41	38.81	32.21	25.61	19.01
3675	3775	104.87	98.27	76.92	70.32	63.72	57.12	50.52	43.92	37.32	30.72	24.12
3775	4025	116.42	109.82	88.47	81.87	75.27	68.67	62.07	55.47	48.87	42.27	35.67
4025	4275	132.92	126.32	104.97	98.37	91.77	85.17	78.57	71.97	65.37	58.77	52.17
4275	4575	151.07	144.47	123.12	116.52	109.92	103.32	96.72	90.12	83.52	76.92	70.32
4575	4975	175.17	168.57	146.22	139.62	133.02	126.42	119.82	113.22	106.62	100.02	93.42
4975	5375	210.37	203.77	177.50	170.90	164.30	157.70	151.10	144.50	137.90	131.30	124.70
5375	5775	245.57	238.97	212.70	206.10	199.50	192.90	186.30	179.70	173.10	166.50	159.90
5775	6225	284.12	277.52	250.10	243.50	236.90	230.30	223.70	217.10	210.50	203.90	197.30
6225	6725	332.71	326.11	296.65	290.05	283.45	276.85	270.25	263.65	257.05	250.45	243.85

6725 and over   (Use Method B - Exact Calculation Method)

California Withholding Schedules For 2024

California Withholding Schedules for 2024

UNMARRIED HEAD OF HOUSEHOLD----SEMI-MONTHLY PAYROLL PERIOD

FOR WAGES PAID IN 2024

IF WAGES ARE...   AND THE NUMBER OF WITHHOLDING ALLOWANCES CLAIMED IS...

AT LEAST	BUT LESS THAN	0	1	2	3	4	5	6	7	8	9	10 OR MORE
		...THE AMOUNT OF INCOME TAX TO BE WITHHELD SHALL BE...										
$1	$600											
600	620	1.79										
620	640	2.01										
640	660	2.23										
660	680	2.45										
680	700	2.67										
700	720	2.89										
720	740	3.11										
740	760	3.33										
760	780	3.55										
780	800	3.77										
800	820	3.99										
820	840	4.21										
840	860	4.43										
860	880	4.65										
880	900	4.87										
900	940	5.20										
940	980	5.64										
980	1020	6.08										
1020	1060	6.52										
1060	1100	6.96	0.36									
1100	1140	7.40	0.80									
1140	1180	7.84	1.24									
1180	1220	8.28	1.68									
1220	1260	8.72	2.12									
1260	1300	9.16	2.56									
1300	1350	9.77	3.17									
1350	1400	10.87	4.27									
1400	1450	11.97	5.37									
1450	1500	13.07	6.47									
1500	1550	14.17	7.57	0.97								
1550	1600	15.27	8.67	2.07								
1600	1650	16.37	9.77	3.17								
1650	1700	17.47	10.87	4.27								
1700	1750	18.57	11.97	5.37								
1750	1800	19.67	13.07	6.47								
1800	1900	21.32	14.72	8.12	1.52							
1900	2000	23.52	16.92	10.32	3.72							
2000	2100	25.72	19.12	12.52	5.92							
2100	2200	27.92	21.32	14.72	8.12	1.52						
2200	2300	30.12	23.52	16.92	10.32	3.72						
2300	2420	32.54	25.94	19.34	12.74	6.14						
2420	2540	35.18	28.58	21.98	15.38	8.78	2.18					
2540	2660	39.93	33.33	26.73	20.13	13.53	6.93	0.33				
2660	2780	45.21	38.61	32.01	25.41	18.81	12.21	5.61				
2780	2900	50.49	43.89	37.29	30.69	24.09	17.49	10.89	4.29			
2900	3230	60.39	53.79	47.19	40.59	33.99	27.39	20.79	14.19	7.59	0.99	
3230	3560	81.43	74.83	68.23	61.63	55.03	48.43	41.83	35.23	28.63	22.03	15.43
3560	3910	104.00	97.40	90.80	84.20	77.60	71.00	64.40	57.80	51.20	44.60	38.00
3910	4260	134.80	128.20	121.60	115.00	108.40	101.80	95.20	88.60	82.00	75.40	68.80
4260	4610	167.19	160.59	153.99	147.39	140.79	134.19	127.59	120.99	114.39	107.79	101.19

4610 and over   (Use Method B - Exact Calculation Method)

California Withholding Schedules for 2024

SINGLE PERSONS, DUAL INCOME MARRIED
OR MARRIED WITH MULTIPLE EMPLOYERS----MONTHLY PAYROLL PERIOD

FOR WAGES PAID IN 2024

IF WAGES ARE...   AND THE NUMBER OF WITHHOLDING ALLOWANCES CLAIMED IS...

AT LEAST	BUT LESS THAN	0	1	2	3	4	5	6	7	8	9	10 OR MORE
		...THE AMOUNT OF INCOME TAX TO BE WITHHELD SHALL BE...										
$1	$600											
600	640	1.90										
640	680	2.34										
680	720	2.78										
720	760	3.22										
760	800	3.66										
800	840	4.10										
840	880	4.54										
880	920	4.98										
920	960	5.42										
960	1000	5.86										
1000	1050	6.36										
1050	1100	6.91										
1100	1150	7.46										
1150	1200	8.01										
1200	1250	8.56										
1250	1300	9.11										
1300	1350	9.77										
1350	1400	10.87										
1400	1450	11.97										
1450	1500	13.07										
1500	1600	14.72	1.52									
1600	1700	16.92	3.72									
1700	1800	19.12	5.92									
1800	1900	21.32	8.12									
1900	2000	23.52	10.32									
2000	2100	25.72	12.52									
2100	2200	27.92	14.72	1.52								
2200	2300	30.12	16.92	3.72								
2300	2400	32.32	19.12	5.92								
2400	2500	34.52	21.32	8.12								
2500	2600	37.71	24.51	11.31								
2600	2700	42.11	28.91	15.71	2.51							
2700	2800	46.51	33.31	20.11	6.91							
2800	2900	50.91	37.71	24.51	11.31							
2900	3000	55.31	42.11	28.91	15.71	2.51						
3000	3100	59.71	46.51	33.31	20.11	6.91						
3100	3200	64.11	50.91	37.71	24.51	11.31						
3200	3300	68.51	55.31	42.11	28.91	15.71	2.51					
3300	3400	72.91	59.71	46.51	33.31	20.11	6.91					
3400	3500	77.31	64.11	50.91	37.71	24.51	11.31					
3500	3700	83.91	70.71	57.51	44.31	31.11	17.91	4.71				
3700	3900	95.07	81.87	68.67	55.47	42.27	29.07	15.87	2.67			
3900	4100	108.27	95.07	81.87	68.67	55.47	42.27	29.07	15.87	2.67		
4100	4400	124.77	111.57	98.37	85.17	71.97	58.77	45.57	32.37	19.17	5.97	
4400	4700	144.57	131.37	118.17	104.97	91.77	78.57	65.37	52.17	38.97	25.77	12.57
4700	5100	167.67	154.47	141.27	128.07	114.87	101.67	88.47	75.27	62.07	48.87	35.67
5100	5575	205.00	191.80	178.60	165.40	152.20	139.00	125.80	112.60	99.40	86.20	73.00
5575	6075	247.90	234.70	221.50	208.30	195.10	181.90	168.70	155.50	142.30	129.10	115.90
6075	6575	294.51	281.31	268.11	254.91	241.71	228.51	215.31	202.11	188.91	175.71	162.51

6575 and over   (Use Method B - Exact Calculation Method)

California Withholding Schedules for 2024

MARRIED PERSONS----MONTHLY PAYROLL PERIOD

FOR WAGES PAID IN 2024

IF WAGES ARE...   AND THE NUMBER OF WITHHOLDING ALLOWANCES CLAIMED IS...

AT LEAST	BUT LESS THAN	0	1	2	3	4	5	6	7	8	9	10 OR MORE
				...THE AMOUNT OF INCOME TAX TO BE WITHHELD SHALL BE...								
$1	$600											
600	640	1.90										
640	680	2.34										
680	720	2.78										
720	760	3.22										
760	800	3.66										
800	840	4.10										
840	880	4.54										
880	920	4.98										
920	960	5.42										
960	1000	5.86										
1000	1040	6.30										
1040	1080	6.74										
1080	1120	7.18										
1120	1160	7.62										
1160	1200	8.06										
1200	1240	8.50										
1240	1280	8.94										
1280	1320	9.38										
1320	1360	9.82										
1360	1400	10.26										
1400	1440	10.70										
1440	1480	11.14										
1480	1520	11.58										
1520	1560	12.02										
1560	1600	12.46										
1600	1640	12.90										
1640	1680	13.34	0.14									
1680	1720	13.78	0.58									
1720	1760	14.22	1.02									
1760	1800	14.66	1.46									
1800	1840	15.10	1.90									
1840	1880	15.54	2.34									
1880	1920	15.98	2.78									
1920	1960	16.42	3.22									
1960	2000	16.86	3.66									
2000	2040	17.30	4.10									
2040	2080	17.74	4.54									
2080	2140	18.29	5.09									
2140	2200	18.95	5.75									
2200	2260	20.13	6.93									
2260	2320	21.45	8.25									
2320	2380	22.77	9.57									
2380	2440	24.09	10.89									
2440	2500	25.41	12.21									
2500	2560	26.73	13.53									
2560	2620	28.05	14.85									
2620	2680	29.37	16.17									
2680	2740	30.69	17.49									
2740	2800	32.01	18.81									
2800	2860	33.33	20.13									

--- CONTINUED NEXT PAGE ---

California Withholding Schedules for 2024

MARRIED PERSONS----MONTHLY PAYROLL PERIOD

FOR WAGES PAID IN 2024

IF WAGES ARE...   AND THE NUMBER OF WITHHOLDING ALLOWANCES CLAIMED IS...

AT LEAST	BUT LESS THAN	0	1	2	3	4	5	6	7	8	9	10 OR MORE
					...THE AMOUNT OF INCOME TAX TO BE WITHHELD SHALL BE...							
2860	2920	34.65	21.45	0.00								
2920	2980	35.97	22.77	0.00								
2980	3040	37.29	24.09	1.06								
3040	3100	38.61	25.41	2.38								
3100	3160	39.93	26.73	3.70								
3160	3220	41.25	28.05	5.02								
3220	3280	42.57	29.37	6.34								
3280	3340	43.89	30.69	7.66								
3340	3400	45.21	32.01	8.98								
3400	3460	46.53	33.33	10.30								
3460	3520	47.85	34.65	11.62								
3520	3580	49.17	35.97	12.94								
3580	3640	50.49	37.29	14.26	1.06							
3640	3700	51.81	38.61	15.58	2.38							
3700	3800	53.57	40.37	17.34	4.14							
3800	3900	55.77	42.57	19.54	6.34							
3900	4000	57.97	44.77	21.74	8.54							
4000	4100	60.17	46.97	23.94	10.74							
4100	4200	62.37	49.17	26.14	12.94							
4200	4300	64.57	51.37	28.34	15.14	1.94						
4300	4400	66.77	53.57	30.54	17.34	4.14						
4400	4500	68.97	55.77	32.74	19.54	6.34						
4500	4600	71.17	57.97	34.94	21.74	8.54						
4600	4700	75.29	62.09	37.14	23.94	10.74						
4700	4800	79.69	66.49	39.34	26.14	12.94						
4800	4900	84.09	70.89	41.54	28.34	15.14	1.94					
4900	5000	88.49	75.29	43.74	30.54	17.34	4.14					
5000	5100	92.89	79.69	46.82	33.62	20.42	7.22					
5100	5200	97.29	84.09	51.22	38.02	24.82	11.62					
5200	5300	101.69	88.49	55.62	42.42	29.22	16.02	2.82				
5300	5400	106.09	92.89	60.02	46.82	33.62	20.42	7.22				
5400	5500	110.49	97.29	64.42	51.22	38.02	24.82	11.62				
5500	5600	114.89	101.69	68.82	55.62	42.42	29.22	16.02	2.82			
5600	5700	119.29	106.09	73.22	60.02	46.82	33.62	20.42	7.22			
5700	5800	123.69	110.49	77.62	64.42	51.22	38.02	24.82	11.62			
5800	5900	128.09	114.89	82.02	68.82	55.62	42.42	29.22	16.02	2.82		
5900	6000	132.49	119.29	86.42	73.22	60.02	46.82	33.62	20.42	7.22		
6000	6200	139.09	125.89	93.02	79.82	66.62	53.42	40.22	27.02	13.82	0.62	
6200	6400	147.89	134.69	101.82	88.62	75.42	62.22	49.02	35.82	22.62	9.42	
6400	6600	156.69	143.49	110.62	97.42	84.22	71.02	57.82	44.62	31.42	18.22	5.02
6600	6800	165.49	152.29	119.42	106.22	93.02	79.82	66.62	53.42	40.22	27.02	13.82
6800	7000	174.29	161.09	128.22	115.02	101.82	88.62	75.42	62.22	49.02	35.82	22.62
7000	7200	186.63	173.43	137.02	123.82	110.62	97.42	84.22	71.02	57.82	44.62	31.42
7200	7400	199.83	186.63	145.82	132.62	119.42	106.22	93.02	79.82	66.62	53.42	40.22
7400	7600	213.03	199.83	157.13	143.93	130.73	117.53	104.33	91.13	77.93	64.73	51.53
7600	7800	226.23	213.03	170.33	157.13	143.93	130.73	117.53	104.33	91.13	77.93	64.73
7800	8100	242.73	229.53	186.83	173.63	160.43	147.23	134.03	120.83	107.63	94.43	81.23
8100	8500	265.83	252.63	209.93	196.73	183.53	170.33	157.13	143.93	130.73	117.53	104.33
8500	8900	292.23	279.03	236.33	223.13	209.93	196.73	183.53	170.33	157.13	143.93	130.73
8900	9450	323.58	310.38	267.68	254.48	241.28	228.08	214.88	201.68	188.48	175.28	162.08
9450	10000	365.74	352.54	303.98	290.78	277.58	264.38	251.18	237.98	224.78	211.58	198.38
10000	10700	420.74	407.54	355.01	341.81	328.61	315.41	302.21	289.01	275.81	262.61	249.41
10700	11400	482.34	469.14	416.61	403.41	390.21	377.01	363.81	350.61	337.41	324.21	311.01
11400	12150	546.14	532.94	480.41	467.21	454.01	440.81	427.61	414.41	401.21	388.01	374.81
12150	12900	621.95	608.75	549.83	536.63	523.43	510.23	497.03	483.83	470.63	457.43	444.23

12900 and over   (Use Method B - Exact Calculation Method)

California Withholding Schedules For 2024

California Withholding Schedules for 2024

UNMARRIED HEAD OF HOUSEHOLD----MONTHLY PAYROLL PERIOD

FOR WAGES PAID IN 2024

IF WAGES ARE...   AND THE NUMBER OF WITHHOLDING ALLOWANCES CLAIMED IS...

AT LEAST	BUT LESS THAN	0	1	2	3	4	5	6	7	8	9	10 OR MORE
					...THE AMOUNT OF INCOME TAX TO BE WITHHELD SHALL BE...							
$1	1400											
1400	1450	5.84										
1450	1500	6.39										
1500	1550	6.94										
1550	1600	7.49										
1600	1650	8.04										
1650	1700	8.59										
1700	1750	9.14										
1750	1800	9.69										
1800	1850	10.24										
1850	1900	10.79										
1900	1950	11.34										
1950	2000	11.89										
2000	2050	12.44										
2050	2100	12.99										
2100	2150	13.54	0.34									
2150	2200	14.09	0.89									
2200	2250	14.64	1.44									
2250	2300	15.19	1.99									
2300	2350	15.74	2.54									
2350	2400	16.29	3.09									
2400	2450	16.84	3.64									
2450	2500	17.39	4.19									
2500	2600	18.22	5.02									
2600	2700	19.54	6.34									
2700	2800	21.74	8.54									
2800	2900	23.94	10.74									
2900	3000	26.14	12.94									
3000	3100	28.34	15.14	1.94								
3100	3200	30.54	17.34	4.14								
3200	3300	32.74	19.54	6.34								
3300	3400	34.94	21.74	8.54								
3400	3500	37.14	23.94	10.74								
3500	3600	39.34	26.14	12.94								
3600	3700	41.54	28.34	15.14	1.94							
3700	3800	43.74	30.54	17.34	4.14							
3800	3900	45.94	32.74	19.54	6.34							
3900	4000	48.14	34.94	21.74	8.54							
4000	4100	50.34	37.14	23.94	10.74							
4100	4200	52.54	39.34	26.14	12.94							
4200	4300	54.74	41.54	28.34	15.14	1.94						
4300	4500	58.04	44.84	31.64	18.44	5.24						
4500	4700	62.44	49.24	36.04	22.84	9.64						
4700	4900	66.84	53.64	40.44	27.24	14.04	0.84					
4900	5100	71.24	58.04	44.84	31.64	18.44	5.24					
5100	5300	79.87	66.67	53.47	40.27	27.07	13.87	0.67				
5300	5600	90.87	77.67	64.47	51.27	38.07	24.87	11.67				
5600	5900	104.07	90.87	77.67	64.47	51.27	38.07	24.87	11.67			
5900	6300	119.47	106.27	93.07	79.87	66.67	53.47	40.27	27.07	13.87	0.67	
6300	6700	143.71	130.51	117.31	104.11	90.91	77.71	64.51	51.31	38.11	24.91	11.71
6700	7250	175.06	161.86	148.66	135.46	122.26	109.06	95.86	82.66	69.46	56.26	43.06
7250	7900	217.24	204.04	190.84	177.64	164.44	151.24	138.04	124.84	111.64	98.44	85.24
7900	8550	274.44	261.24	248.04	234.84	221.64	208.44	195.24	182.04	168.84	155.64	142.44
8550	9200	334.89	321.69	308.49	295.29	282.09	268.89	255.69	242.49	229.29	216.09	202.89

9200 and over   (Use Method B - Exact Calculation Method)

California Withholding Schedules For 2024

California Withholding Schedules for 2024

SINGLE PERSONS, DUAL INCOME MARRIED
OR MARRIED WITH MULTIPLE EMPLOYERS----DAILY / MISCELLANEOUS PAYROLL PERIOD

FOR WAGES PAID IN 2024

IF WAGES ARE...   AND THE NUMBER OF WITHHOLDING ALLOWANCES CLAIMED IS...

AT LEAST	BUT LESS THAN	0	1	2	3	4	5	6	7	8	9	10 OR MORE
					...THE AMOUNT OF INCOME TAX TO BE WITHHELD SHALL BE...							
$1	$28											
28	30	0.09										
30	32	0.11										
32	34	0.14										
34	36	0.16										
36	38	0.18										
38	40	0.20										
40	42	0.22										
42	44	0.25										
44	46	0.27										
46	48	0.29										
48	50	0.31										
50	54	0.35										
54	58	0.39										
58	62	0.43										
62	66	0.51										
66	70	0.60										
70	74	0.69	0.09									
74	78	0.78	0.17									
78	82	0.87	0.26									
82	86	0.95	0.35									
86	90	1.04	0.44									
90	94	1.13	0.53									
94	98	1.22	0.61	0.01								
98	102	1.31	0.70	0.10								
102	106	1.39	0.79	0.18								
106	110	1.48	0.88	0.27								
110	114	1.57	0.97	0.36								
114	118	1.67	1.06	0.46								
118	122	1.84	1.24	0.63	0.03							
122	126	2.02	1.41	0.81	0.20							
126	131	2.22	1.61	1.01	0.40							
131	136	2.44	1.83	1.23	0.62	0.02						
136	141	2.66	2.05	1.45	0.84	0.24						
141	146	2.88	2.27	1.67	1.06	0.46						
146	151	3.10	2.49	1.89	1.28	0.68	0.07					
151	156	3.32	2.71	2.11	1.50	0.90	0.29					
156	161	3.54	2.93	2.33	1.72	1.12	0.51					
161	166	3.76	3.15	2.55	1.94	1.34	0.73	0.13				
166	171	3.98	3.37	2.77	2.16	1.56	0.95	0.35				
171	176	4.26	3.65	3.05	2.44	1.84	1.23	0.63	0.02			
176	181	4.59	3.98	3.38	2.77	2.17	1.56	0.96	0.35			
181	186	4.92	4.31	3.71	3.10	2.50	1.89	1.29	0.68	0.08		
186	201	5.58	4.97	4.37	3.76	3.16	2.55	1.95	1.34	0.74	0.13	
201	226	6.90	6.29	5.69	5.08	4.48	3.87	3.27	2.66	2.06	1.45	0.85
226	251	8.77	8.16	7.56	6.95	6.35	5.74	5.14	4.53	3.93	3.32	2.72
251	281	11.19	10.58	9.98	9.37	8.77	8.16	7.56	6.95	6.35	5.74	5.14
281	311	14.00	13.40	12.79	12.19	11.58	10.98	10.37	9.77	9.16	8.56	7.95

321 and over   (Use Method B - Exact Calculation Method)

California Withholding Schedules for 2024

MARRIED PERSONS----DAILY / MISCELLANEOUS PAYROLL PERIOD

FOR WAGES PAID IN 2024

IF WAGES ARE...   AND THE NUMBER OF WITHHOLDING ALLOWANCES CLAIMED IS...

AT LEAST	BUT LESS THAN	0	1	2	3	4	5	6	7	8	9	10 OR MORE
					...THE AMOUNT OF INCOME TAX TO BE WITHHELD SHALL BE...							
$1	$32											
32	34	0.14										
34	36	0.16										
36	38	0.18										
38	40	0.20										
40	42	0.22										
42	44	0.25										
44	46	0.27										
46	48	0.29										
48	50	0.31										
50	52	0.33										
		0.00										
52	54	0.36										
54	56	0.38										
56	58	0.40										
58	60	0.42										
60	62	0.44										
62	64	0.47										
64	66	0.49										
66	68	0.51										
68	70	0.53										
70	72	0.55										
72	74	0.58										
74	76	0.60										
76	78	0.62	0.02									
78	80	0.64	0.04									
80	82	0.66	0.06									
82	84	0.69	0.08									
84	86	0.71	0.10									
86	88	0.73	0.13									
88	90	0.75	0.15									
90	92	0.77	0.17									
92	94	0.80	0.19									
94	96	0.82	0.21									
96	98	0.84	0.24									
98	100	0.86	0.26									
100	102	0.89	0.28									
102	104	0.93	0.33									
104	106	0.98	0.37									
106	108	1.02	0.42									
108	110	1.06	0.46									
110	112	1.11	0.50									
112	114	1.15	0.55									
114	118	1.22	0.61	0.01								
118	122	1.31	0.70	0.10								
122	126	1.39	0.79	0.18								
126	130	1.48	0.88	0.27								
130	134	1.57	0.97	0.36								
134	138	1.66	1.05	0.45								
138	142	1.75	1.14	0.54								
142	146	1.83	1.23	0.62	0.02							
146	150	1.92	1.32	0.71	0.11							

--- CONTINUED NEXT PAGE ---

California Withholding Schedules for 2024

MARRIED PERSONS----DAILY / MISCELLANEOUS PAYROLL PERIOD

FOR WAGES PAID IN 2024

IF WAGES ARE... AND THE NUMBER OF WITHHOLDING ALLOWANCES CLAIMED IS...

AT LEAST	BUT LESS THAN	0	1	2	3	4	5	6	7	8	9	10 OR MORE
		...THE AMOUNT OF INCOME TAX TO BE WITHHELD SHALL BE...										
150	154	2.01	1.41	0.80	0.20							
154	158	2.10	1.49	0.89	0.28							
158	162	2.19	1.58	0.98	0.37							
162	166	2.27	1.67	1.06	0.46							
166	170	2.36	1.76	1.15	0.55							
170	174	2.45	1.85	1.24	0.64	0.03						
174	178	2.54	1.93	1.33	0.72	0.12						
178	182	2.63	2.02	1.42	0.81	0.21						
182	186	2.71	2.11	1.50	0.90	0.29						
186	190	2.80	2.20	1.59	0.99	0.38						
190	195	2.90	2.30	1.69	1.09	0.48						
195	200	3.01	2.41	1.80	1.20	0.59						
200	205	3.12	2.52	1.91	1.31	0.70	0.10					
205	210	3.23	2.63	2.02	1.42	0.81	0.21					
210	215	3.38	2.78	2.17	1.57	0.96	0.36					
215	220	3.60	3.00	2.39	1.79	1.18	0.58					
220	225	3.82	3.22	2.61	2.01	1.40	0.80	0.19				
225	230	4.04	3.44	2.83	2.23	1.62	1.02	0.41				
230	235	4.26	3.66	3.05	2.45	1.84	1.24	0.63	0.03			
235	240	4.48	3.88	3.27	2.67	2.06	1.46	0.85	0.25			
240	245	4.70	4.10	3.49	2.89	2.28	1.68	1.07	0.47			
245	250	4.92	4.32	3.71	3.11	2.50	1.90	1.29	0.69	0.08		
250	255	5.14	4.54	3.93	3.33	2.72	2.12	1.51	0.91	0.30		
255	260	5.36	4.76	4.15	3.55	2.94	2.34	1.73	1.13	0.52		
260	265	5.58	4.98	4.37	3.77	3.16	2.56	1.95	1.35	0.74	0.14	
265	270	5.80	5.20	4.59	3.99	3.38	2.78	2.17	1.57	0.96	0.36	
270	275	6.02	5.42	4.81	4.21	3.60	3.00	2.39	1.79	1.18	0.58	
275	280	6.24	5.64	5.03	4.43	3.82	3.22	2.61	2.01	1.40	0.80	0.19
280	285	6.46	5.86	5.25	4.65	4.04	3.44	2.83	2.23	1.62	1.02	0.41
285	290	6.68	6.08	5.47	4.87	4.26	3.66	3.05	2.45	1.84	1.24	0.63
290	300	7.01	6.41	5.80	5.20	4.59	3.99	3.38	2.78	2.17	1.57	0.96
300	310	7.45	6.85	6.24	5.64	5.03	4.43	3.82	3.22	2.61	2.01	1.40
310	320	7.89	7.29	6.68	6.08	5.47	4.87	4.26	3.66	3.05	2.45	1.84
320	330	8.43	7.82	7.22	6.61	6.01	5.40	4.80	4.19	3.59	2.98	2.38
330	340	9.09	8.48	7.88	7.27	6.67	6.06	5.46	4.85	4.25	3.64	3.04
340	350	9.75	9.14	8.54	7.93	7.33	6.72	6.12	5.51	4.91	4.30	3.70
350	360	10.41	9.80	9.20	8.59	7.99	7.38	6.78	6.17	5.57	4.96	4.36
360	380	11.40	10.79	10.19	9.58	8.98	8.37	7.77	7.16	6.56	5.95	5.35
380	400	12.72	12.11	11.51	10.90	10.30	9.69	9.09	8.48	7.88	7.27	6.67
400	425	14.20	13.60	12.99	12.39	11.78	11.18	10.57	9.97	9.36	8.76	8.15
425	460	16.31	15.71	15.10	14.50	13.89	13.29	12.68	12.08	11.47	10.87	10.26
460	500	19.61	19.01	18.40	17.80	17.19	16.59	15.98	15.38	14.77	14.17	13.56
500	540	23.13	22.53	21.92	21.32	20.71	20.11	19.50	18.90	18.29	17.69	17.08
540	580	26.84	26.24	25.63	25.03	24.42	23.82	23.21	22.61	22.00	21.40	20.79

580 and over (Use Method B - Exact Calculation Method)

California Withholding Schedules for 2024

UNMARRIED HEAD OF HOUSEHOLD----DAILY / MISCELLANEOUS PAYROLL PERIOD

FOR WAGES PAID IN 2024

IF WAGES ARE...		AND THE NUMBER OF WITHHOLDING ALLOWANCES CLAIMED IS...										
AT LEAST	BUT LESS THAN	0	1	2	3	4	5	6	7	8	9	10 OR MORE
		...THE AMOUNT OF INCOME TAX TO BE WITHHELD SHALL BE...										
$1	$56											
56	58	0.17										
58	60	0.20										
60	62	0.22										
62	64	0.24										
64	66	0.26										
66	68	0.28										
68	70	0.31										
70	72	0.33										
72	74	0.35										
74	76	0.37										
76	78	0.39										
78	80	0.42										
80	82	0.44										
82	84	0.46										
84	86	0.48										
86	88	0.50										
88	90	0.53										
90	92	0.55										
92	94	0.57										
94	96	0.59										
96	100	0.62	0.02									
100	104	0.67	0.06									
104	108	0.71	0.11									
108	112	0.76	0.15									
112	116	0.80	0.20									
116	121	0.85	0.24									
121	126	0.93	0.32									
126	131	1.04	0.43									
131	136	1.15	0.54									
136	141	1.26	0.65	0.05								
141	146	1.37	0.76	0.16								
146	151	1.48	0.87	0.27								
151	156	1.59	0.98	0.38								
156	161	1.70	1.09	0.49								
161	166	1.81	1.20	0.60								
166	171	1.92	1.31	0.71	0.10							
171	176	2.03	1.42	0.82	0.21							
176	181	2.14	1.53	0.93	0.32							
181	186	2.25	1.64	1.04	0.43							
186	191	2.36	1.75	1.15	0.54							
191	196	2.47	1.86	1.26	0.65	0.05						
196	206	2.63	2.03	1.42	0.82	0.21						
206	216	2.85	2.25	1.64	1.04	0.43						
216	226	3.07	2.47	1.86	1.26	0.65	0.05					
226	236	3.29	2.69	2.08	1.48	0.87	0.27					
236	246	3.73	3.12	2.52	1.91	1.31	0.70	0.10				
246	256	4.17	3.56	2.96	2.35	1.75	1.14	0.54				
256	276	4.83	4.22	3.62	3.01	2.41	1.80	1.20	0.59			
276	296	5.71	5.10	4.50	3.89	3.29	2.68	2.08	1.47	0.87	0.26	
296	326	7.35	6.75	6.14	5.54	4.93	4.33	3.72	3.12	2.51	1.91	1.30
326	361	9.50	8.89	8.29	7.68	7.08	6.47	5.87	5.26	4.66	4.05	3.45
361	396	12.56	11.96	11.35	10.75	10.14	9.54	8.93	8.33	7.72	7.12	6.51
396	431	15.84	15.24	14.63	14.03	13.42	12.82	12.21	11.61	11.00	10.40	9.79

431 and over   (Use Method B - Exact Calculation Method)

California Withholding Schedules For 2024

California Withholding Schedules for 2024

Method B – Exact Calculation Method

This method is based upon applying a given percentage to the wages (after deductions) which fall within a taxable income class, adding to this product the accumulated tax for all lower tax brackets; and then subtracting a tax credit based upon the number of allowances claimed on the *Employee's Withholding Allowance Certificate* (Form W-4 or DE 4). **This method also takes into consideration the special treatment of additional allowances for estimated deductions.**

The steps in computing the amount of tax to be withheld are as follows:

Step 1   Determine if the employee's gross wages are **less** than, or equal to, the amount shown in Table 1 – Low Income Exemption Table. If so, no income tax is required to be withheld.

Step 2   If the employee claims any additional withholding allowances for estimated deductions on a DE 4 form, subtract the amount shown in Table 2 – Estimated Deduction Table from the gross wages.

Step 3   Subtract the standard deduction amount shown in Table 3 – Standard Deduction Table to arrive at the employee's taxable income.

Step 4   Use Table 5 – Tax Rate Table for the payroll period and marital status to find the applicable line on which the taxable income is located. Perform the indicated calculations to arrive at the computed tax liability.

Step 5   Subtract the tax credit shown in Table 4 – Exemption Allowance Table* from the computed tax liability to arrive at the amount of tax to be withheld.

          *If the employee uses additional allowances claimed for estimated deductions, such allowances **MUST NOT** be used in the determination of tax credits to be subtracted.

Example A: Weekly earnings of $210, single, and claiming one withholding allowance on Form W-4 or DE 4.

Step 1   Earnings for the weekly payroll period are LESS than the amount shown in Table 1 – Low Income Exemption Table ($342); therefore, no income tax is to be withheld.

Example B: Biweekly earnings of $1,600, married, and claiming three withholding allowances, one of which is for estimated deductions.

Step 1   Earnings for the biweekly payroll period are *greater* than the amount shown in Table 1 – Low Income Exemption Table ($1,367); therefore, income tax should be withheld.

Step 2
Earnings for biweekly payroll period.	$1,600.00
Subtract amount from Table 2 – Estimated Deduction Table.	-38.00
Salaries and wages subject to withholding.	$1,562.00

Step 3
Subtract amount from Table 3 – Standard Deduction Table.	-413.00
Taxable income.	$1,149.00

Step 4   Tax computation from Table 5 – Tax Rate Table:
Entry covering $1,149 (over $800 but not over $1,900).

• 2.2% amount over $800 (.022 x ($1,149 – $800)).	$ 7.68
• Plus the marginal amount.	+8.80
• Computed tax.	16.48

Step 5
Subtract amount from Table 4 – Exemption Allowance Table. for two regular withholding allowances.	-12.18
Net amount of tax to be withheld.	$ 4.30

NOTE: Table 5 provides a method comparable to the federal alternative method for percentage calculation of withholding. This method is a minor simplification of the exact calculation method described above in that the tax rate applies to the total taxable income with the excess amount subtracted.

California Withholding Schedules for 2024

Method B – Exact Calculation Method Continued

Example C: Monthly earnings of $5,100 married, and claiming five withholding allowances on Form W-4 or DE 4.

Step 1	Earnings for the monthly payroll period are *greater* than the amount shown in Table 1 – Low Income Exemption Table ($2,962) therefore, income tax should be withheld.	
Step 2	Earnings for monthly payroll period.	$ 5,100.00
	Not applicable - no estimated deduction allowance claimed.	
Step 3	Subtract amount from Table 3 – Standard Deduction Table.	-894.00
	Taxable income.	$ 4,206.00
Step 4	Tax computation from Table 5 – Tax Rate Table:	
	• Entry covering $4,206 (over $4,116 but not over $6,492).	
	• 4.4% of amount over $4,116 (.044 x ($4,206 - $4,116)).	$ 3.96
	• Plus marginal tax amount.	+71.46
	• Computed tax.	$ 75.42
Step 5	Subtract amount from Table 4 – Exemption Allowance Table for 5 regular withholding allowances.	-66.00
	Net amount of tax to be withheld.	$ 9.42

Example D: Weekly earnings of $850, unmarried head of household, and three withholding allowances on Form W-4 or DE 4.

Step 1	Earnings for the weekly payroll period are *greater* than the amount shown in Table 1 – Low Income Exemption Table ($683); therefore, income tax should be withheld.	
Step 2	Earnings for weekly payroll period.	$ 850.00
	Not applicable - no estimated deduction allowance claimed.	
Step 3	Subtract amount from Table 3 – Standard Deduction Table.	-206.00
	Taxable income.	$ 644.00
Step 4	Tax computation from Table 5 – Tax Rate Table:	
	• Entry covering $644 (over $401 but not over $949).	
	• 2.2% of amount over $401 (.022 x ($644 - $401)).	$ 5.35
	• Plus marginal tax amount.	+ 4.41
	• Computed tax.	$ 9.76
Step 5	Subtract amount from Table 4 – Exemption Allowance Table for 3 regular withholding allowances.	- 9.14
	Net amount of tax to be withheld.	$ 0.62

Example E: Semi-monthly earnings of $2,100, married, and claiming four allowances on Form W-4 or DE 4.

Step 1	Earnings for the semi-monthly payroll period are *greater* than the amount shown in Table 1 – Low Income Exemption Table ($1,481); therefore, income tax should be withheld.	
Step 2	Annualized wages and salary (24 x $2,100).	$ 50,400.00
	Not applicable - no estimated deduction allowance claimed.	
Step 3	Subtract amount from Table 3 – Standard Deduction Table.	-10,726.00
	Taxable income.	$ 39,674.00
Step 4	Tax computation from Table 5 – Tax Rate Table:	
	• Entry covering $39,674 (over $20,824 but not over $49,368).	
	• 2.2% of amount over $20,824 (.022 x ($39,674- $20,824)).	$ 414.70
	• Plus marginal tax amount.	+229.06
	• Computed annual tax.	$ 643.76
Step 5	Subtract amount from Table 4 – Exemption Allowance Table for 4 regular withholding allowances.	-633.60
	Annual amount of tax to be withheld.	$ 10.16
	Divide by number of payroll periods in year (24).	$ 0.42

NOTE: Employers may determine the amount of income tax to be withheld for an annual payroll period and prorate the tax back to the payroll period. This method may be useful to employers who have employees being paid for more than one payroll period and want to conserve computer memory by storing only the annual tax rates, wage brackets, deduction values, and tax credits.

California Withholding Schedules for 2024

Method B – Exact Calculation Method Continued

Example F: Annual earnings of $57,000, monthly pay period, married, and claiming four allowances on Form W-4 or DE 4.

Step 1	Earnings for the annual payroll period are *greater* than the amount shown in Table 1 – Low Income Exemption Table ($35,538); therefore, income tax should be withheld.	
Step 2	Annualized wages and/or monthly salary (12 x $4,750).	$ 57,000.00
	Not applicable - no estimated deduction allowance claimed.	
Step 3	Subtract amount from Table 3 – Standard Deduction Table.	-10,726.00
	Taxable income.	$ 46,274.00
Step 4	Tax computation from Table 5 – Tax Rate Table:	
	• Entry covering $46,274 (over $20,824 but not over $49,368).	
	• 2.2% of amount over $20,824 (.022 x ($46,274 - $20,824)).	$ 559.90
	• Plus marginal tax amount.	+229.06
	• Computed annual tax.	$ 788.96
Step 5	Subtract amount from Table 4 – Exemption Allowance Table for 4 regular withholding allowances.	-633.60
	Annual amount of tax to be withheld.	$ 155.36
	Divide by number of payroll periods in year (12).	$ 12.95

NOTE: Employers may determine the amount of income tax to be withheld for an annual payroll period and figure the tax for the payroll period. This method may be useful to employers who have employees being paid for a lump sum, or a yearly amount not withheld on; and want to conserve computer memory by storing only the annual tax rates, wage brackets, deduction values, and tax credits.

California Withholding Schedules for 2024

METHOD B---EXACT CALCULATION METHOD

TABLE 1 - LOW INCOME EXEMPTION TABLE

PAYROLL PERIOD	SINGLE, DUAL INCOME MARRIED OR MARRIED WITH MULTIPLE EMPLOYERS	MARRIED		UNMARRIED HEAD OF HOUSEHOLD
		ALLOWANCES ON DE 4 OR FORM W-4		
		"0" OR "1"	"2" OR MORE	
WEEKLY	$342	$342	$683	$683
BIWEEKLY	$683	$683	$1,367	$1,367
SEMI-MONTHLY	$740	$740	$1,481	$1,481
MONTHLY	$1,481	$1,481	$2,962	$2,962
QUARTERLY	$4,442	$4,442	$8,885	$8,885
SEMI-ANNUAL	$8,885	$8,885	$17,769	$17,769
ANNUAL	$17,769	$17,769	$35,538	$35,538
DAILY/MISCELLANEOUS	$68	$68	$137	$137

TABLE 2 - ESTIMATED DEDUCTION TABLE

ADDITIONAL WITHHOLDING ALLOWANCES *	PAYROLL PERIOD							
	WEEKLY	BI-WEEKLY	SEMI-MONTHLY	MONTHLY	QUARTERLY	SEMI-ANNUAL	ANNUAL	DAILY/MISC.
1	$19	$38	$42	$83	$250	$500	$1,000	$4
2	$38	$77	$83	$167	$500	$1,000	$2,000	$8
3	$58	$115	$125	$250	$750	$1,500	$3,000	$12
4	$77	$154	$167	$333	$1,000	$2,000	$4,000	$15
5	$96	$192	$208	$417	$1,250	$2,500	$5,000	$19
6	$115	$231	$250	$500	$1,500	$3,000	$6,000	$23
7	$135	$269	$292	$583	$1,750	$3,500	$7,000	$27
8	$154	$308	$333	$667	$2,000	$4,000	$8,000	$31
9	$173	$346	$375	$750	$2,250	$4,500	$9,000	$35
10**	$192	$385	$417	$833	$2,500	$5,000	$10,000	$38

*Number of Additional Withholding Allowances for Estimated Deductions claimed on Form W-4 or DE 4.

**If the number of Additional Withholding Allowances for Estimated Deductions claimed is greater than 10, multiply the amount shown for one Additional Allowance by the number claimed.

California Withholding Schedules for 2024

METHOD B---EXACT CALCULATION METHOD

TABLE 3 - STANDARD DEDUCTION TABLE

| PAYROLL PERIOD | SINGLE, DUAL INCOME MARRIED OR MARRIED WITH MULTIPLE EMPLOYERS | MARRIED | | UNMARRIED HEAD OF HOUSEHOLD |
| | | ALLOWANCES ON DE 4 OR FORM W-4 | | |
		'0' OR '1'	'2' OR MORE	
WEEKLY	$103	$103	$206	$206
BIWEEKLY	$206	$206	$413	$413
SEMI-MONTHLY	$223	$223	$447	$447
MONTHLY	$447	$447	$894	$894
QUARTERLY	$1,341	$1,341	$2,682	$2,682
SEMI-ANNUAL	$2,682	$2,682	$5,363	$5,363
ANNUAL	$5,363	$5,363	$10,726	$10,726
DAILY/MISCELLANEOUS	$21	$21	$41	$41

TABLE 4 - EXEMPTION ALLOWANCE TABLE

| ALLOWANCES ON DE 4 OR FORM W-4 | PAYROLL PERIOD | | | | | | | |
	WEEKLY	BI-WEEKLY	SEMI-MONTHLY	MONTHLY	QUARTERLY	SEMI-ANNUAL	ANNUAL	DAILY/MISC.
0	$0.00	$0.00	$0.00	$0.00	$0.00	$0.00	$0.00	$0.00
1	$3.05	$6.09	$6.60	$13.20	$39.60	$79.20	$158.40	$0.61
2	$6.09	$12.18	$13.20	$26.40	$79.20	$158.40	$316.80	$1.22
3	$9.14	$18.28	$19.80	$39.60	$118.80	$237.60	$475.20	$1.83
4	$12.18	$24.37	$26.40	$52.80	$158.40	$316.80	$633.60	$2.44
5	$15.23	$30.46	$33.00	$66.00	$198.00	$396.00	$792.00	$3.05
6	$18.28	$36.55	$39.60	$79.20	$237.60	$475.20	$950.40	$3.66
7	$21.32	$42.65	$46.20	$92.40	$277.20	$554.40	$1,108.80	$4.26
8	$24.37	$48.74	$52.80	$105.60	$316.80	$633.60	$1,267.20	$4.87
9	$27.42	$54.83	$59.40	$118.80	$356.40	$712.80	$1,425.60	$5.48
10*	$30.46	$60.92	$66.00	$132.00	$396.00	$792.00	$1,584.00	$6.09

* If the number of allowances claimed exceeds 10, you may determine the amount of tax credit to be allowed by multiplying the amount for one allowance by the total number of allowances.

For example, the amount of tax credit for a married taxpayer with 15 allowances, as determined on Form W-4 or DE 4. on a weekly payroll period would be $45.75

California Withholding Schedules for 2024

METHOD B---EXACT CALCULATION METHOD

TABLE 5 - TAX RATE TABLE

ANNUAL PAYROLL PERIOD

SINGLE PERSONS, DUAL INCOME MARRIED, OR MARRIED WITH MULTIPLE EMPLOYERS

IF THE TAXABLE INCOME IS...		THE COMPUTED TAX IS...		
OVER	BUT NOT OVER	OF AMOUNT OVER...		PLUS
$0	$10,412 ...	1.100%	$0	$0.00
$10,412	$24,684 ...	2.200%	$10,412	$114.53
$24,684	$38,959 ...	4.400%	$24,684	$428.51
$38,959	$54,081 ...	6.600%	$38,959	$1,056.61
$54,081	$68,350 ...	8.800%	$54,081	$2,054.66
$68,350	$349,137 ...	10.230%	$68,350	$3,310.33
$349,137	$418,961 ...	11.330%	$349,137	$32,034.84
$418,961	$698,271 ...	12.430%	$418,961	$39,945.90
$698,271	$1,000,000 ...	13.530%	$698,271	$74,664.13
$1,000,000	and over ...	14.630%	$1,000,000	$115,488.06

MARRIED PERSONS

IF THE TAXABLE INCOME IS...		THE COMPUTED TAX IS...		
OVER	BUT NOT OVER	OF AMOUNT OVER...		PLUS
$0	$20,824 ...	1.100%	$0	$0.00
$20,824	$49,368 ...	2.200%	$20,824	$229.06
$49,368	$77,918 ...	4.400%	$49,368	$857.03
$77,918	$108,162 ...	6.600%	$77,918	$2,113.23
$108,162	$136,700 ...	8.800%	$108,162	$4,109.33
$136,700	$698,274 ...	10.230%	$136,700	$6,620.67
$698,274	$837,922 ...	11.330%	$698,274	$64,069.69
$837,922	$1,000,000 ...	12.430%	$837,922	$79,891.81
$1,000,000	$1,396,542 ...	13.530%	$1,000,000	$100,038.11
$1,396,542	and over ...	14.630%	$1,396,542	$153,690.24

UNMARRIED/HEAD OF HOUSEHOLD

IF THE TAXABLE INCOME IS...		THE COMPUTED TAX IS...		
OVER	BUT NOT OVER	OF AMOUNT OVER...		PLUS
$0	$20,839 ...	1.100%	$0	$0.00
$20,839	$49,371 ...	2.200%	$20,839	$229.23
$49,371	$63,644 ...	4.400%	$49,371	$856.93
$63,644	$78,765 ...	6.600%	$63,644	$1,484.94
$78,765	$93,037 ...	8.800%	$78,765	$2,482.93
$93,037	$474,824 ...	10.230%	$93,037	$3,738.87
$474,824	$569,790 ...	11.330%	$474,824	$42,795.68
$569,790	$949,649 ...	12.430%	$569,790	$53,555.33
$949,649	$1,000,000 ...	13.530%	$949,649	$100,771.80
$1,000,000	and over ...	14.630%	$1,000,000	$107,584.29

DAILY / MISCELLANEOUS PAYROLL PERIOD

SINGLE PERSONS, DUAL INCOME MARRIED, OR MARRIED WITH MULTIPLE EMPLOYERS

IF THE TAXABLE INCOME IS...		THE COMPUTED TAX IS...		
OVER	BUT NOT OVER	OF AMOUNT OVER...		PLUS
$0	$40 ...	1.100%	$0	$0.00
$40	$95 ...	2.200%	$40	$0.44
$95	$150 ...	4.400%	$95	$1.65
$150	$208 ...	6.600%	$150	$4.07
$208	$263 ...	8.800%	$208	$7.90
$263	$1,343 ...	10.230%	$263	$12.74
$1,343	$1,611 ...	11.330%	$1,343	$123.22
$1,611	$2,686 ...	12.430%	$1,611	$153.58
$2,686	$3,846 ...	13.530%	$2,686	$287.20
$3,846	and over ...	14.630%	$3,846	$444.15

MARRIED PERSONS

IF THE TAXABLE INCOME IS...		THE COMPUTED TAX IS...		
OVER	BUT NOT OVER	OF AMOUNT OVER...		PLUS
$0	$80 ...	1.100%	$0	$0.00
$80	$190 ...	2.200%	$80	$0.88
$190	$300 ...	4.400%	$190	$3.30
$300	$416 ...	6.600%	$300	$8.14
$416	$526 ...	8.800%	$416	$15.80
$526	$2,686 ...	10.230%	$526	$25.48
$2,686	$3,222 ...	11.330%	$2,686	$246.45
$3,222	$3,846 ...	12.430%	$3,222	$307.18
$3,846	$5,371 ...	13.530%	$3,846	$384.74
$5,371	and over ...	14.630%	$5,371	$591.07

UNMARRIED/HEAD OF HOUSEHOLD

IF THE TAXABLE INCOME IS...		THE COMPUTED TAX IS...		
OVER	BUT NOT OVER	OF AMOUNT OVER...		PLUS
$0	$80 ...	1.100%	$0	$0.00
$80	$190 ...	2.200%	$80	$0.88
$190	$245 ...	4.400%	$190	$3.30
$245	$303 ...	6.600%	$245	$5.72
$303	$358 ...	8.800%	$303	$9.55
$358	$1,826 ...	10.230%	$358	$14.39
$1,826	$2,192 ...	11.330%	$1,826	$164.57
$2,192	$3,652 ...	12.430%	$2,192	$206.04
$3,652	$3,846 ...	13.530%	$3,652	$387.52
$3,846	and over ...	14.630%	$3,846	$413.77

California Withholding Schedules For 2024

California Withholding Schedules for 2024

METHOD B---EXACT CALCULATION METHOD

TABLE 5 - TAX RATE TABLE

QUARTERLY PAYROLL PERIOD

SINGLE PERSONS, DUAL INCOME MARRIED, OR MARRIED WITH MULTIPLE EMPLOYERS

IF THE TAXABLE INCOME IS...		THE COMPUTED TAX IS...		
OVER	BUT NOT OVER	OF AMOUNT OVER...		PLUS
$0	$2,603 ...	1.100%	$0	$0.00
$2,603	$6,171 ...	2.200%	$2,603	$28.63
$6,171	$9,740 ...	4.400%	$6,171	$107.13
$9,740	$13,520 ...	6.600%	$9,740	$264.17
$13,520	$17,088 ...	8.800%	$13,520	$513.65
$17,088	$87,284 ...	10.230%	$17,088	$827.63
$87,284	$104,740 ...	11.330%	$87,284	$8,008.68
$104,740	$174,568 ...	12.430%	$104,740	$9,986.44
$174,568	$250,000 ...	13.530%	$174,568	$18,666.06
$250,000	and over ...	14.630%	$250,000	$28,872.01

MARRIED PERSONS

IF THE TAXABLE INCOME IS...		THE COMPUTED TAX IS...		
OVER	BUT NOT OVER	OF AMOUNT OVER...		PLUS
$0	$5,206 ...	1.100%	$0	$0.00
$5,206	$12,342 ...	2.200%	$5,206	$57.27
$12,342	$19,480 ...	4.400%	$12,342	$214.26
$19,480	$27,040 ...	6.600%	$19,480	$528.33
$27,040	$34,176 ...	8.800%	$27,040	$1,027.29
$34,176	$174,568 ...	10.230%	$34,176	$1,655.26
$174,568	$209,480 ...	11.330%	$174,568	$16,017.36
$209,480	$250,000 ...	12.430%	$209,480	$19,972.89
$250,000	$349,136 ...	13.530%	$250,000	$25,009.53
$349,136	and over ...	14.630%	$349,136	$38,422.63

UNMARRIED/HEAD OF HOUSEHOLD

IF THE TAXABLE INCOME IS...		THE COMPUTED TAX IS...		
OVER	BUT NOT OVER	OF AMOUNT OVER...		PLUS
$0	$5,210 ...	1.100%	$0	$0.00
$5,210	$12,343 ...	2.200%	$5,210	$57.31
$12,343	$15,911 ...	4.400%	$12,343	$214.24
$15,911	$19,691 ...	6.600%	$15,911	$371.23
$19,691	$23,259 ...	8.800%	$19,691	$620.71
$23,259	$118,706 ...	10.230%	$23,259	$934.69
$118,706	$142,448 ...	11.330%	$118,706	$10,698.92
$142,448	$237,412 ...	12.430%	$142,448	$13,388.89
$237,412	$250,000 ...	13.530%	$237,412	$25,192.92
$250,000	and over ...	14.630%	$250,000	$26,896.08

SEMI-ANNUAL PAYROLL PERIOD

SINGLE PERSONS, DUAL INCOME MARRIED, OR MARRIED WITH MULTIPLE EMPLOYERS

IF THE TAXABLE INCOME IS...		THE COMPUTED TAX IS...		
OVER	BUT NOT OVER	OF AMOUNT OVER...		PLUS
$0	$5,206 ...	1.100%	$0	$0.00
$5,206	$12,342 ...	2.200%	$5,206	$57.27
$12,342	$19,480 ...	4.400%	$12,342	$214.26
$19,480	$27,040 ...	6.600%	$19,480	$528.33
$27,040	$34,176 ...	8.800%	$27,040	$1,027.29
$34,176	$174,568 ...	10.230%	$34,176	$1,655.26
$174,568	$209,480 ...	11.330%	$174,568	$16,017.36
$209,480	$349,136 ...	12.430%	$209,480	$19,972.89
$349,136	$500,000 ...	13.530%	$349,136	$37,332.13
$500,000	and over ...	14.630%	$500,000	$57,744.03

MARRIED PERSONS

IF THE TAXABLE INCOME IS...		THE COMPUTED TAX IS...		
OVER	BUT NOT OVER	OF AMOUNT OVER...		PLUS
$0	$10,412 ...	1.100%	$0	$0.00
$10,412	$24,684 ...	2.200%	$10,412	$114.53
$24,684	$38,960 ...	4.400%	$24,684	$428.51
$38,960	$54,080 ...	6.600%	$38,960	$1,056.65
$54,080	$68,352 ...	8.800%	$54,080	$2,054.57
$68,352	$349,136 ...	10.230%	$68,352	$3,310.51
$349,136	$418,960 ...	11.330%	$349,136	$32,034.71
$418,960	$500,000 ...	12.430%	$418,960	$39,945.77
$500,000	$698,272 ...	13.530%	$500,000	$50,019.04
$698,272	and over ...	14.630%	$698,272	$76,845.24

UNMARRIED/HEAD OF HOUSEHOLD

IF THE TAXABLE INCOME IS...		THE COMPUTED TAX IS...		
OVER	BUT NOT OVER	OF AMOUNT OVER...		PLUS
$0	$10,420 ...	1.100%	$0	$0.00
$10,420	$24,686 ...	2.200%	$10,420	$114.62
$24,686	$31,822 ...	4.400%	$24,686	$428.47
$31,822	$39,382 ...	6.600%	$31,822	$742.45
$39,382	$46,518 ...	8.800%	$39,382	$1,241.41
$46,518	$237,412 ...	10.230%	$46,518	$1,869.38
$237,412	$284,896 ...	11.330%	$237,412	$21,397.84
$284,896	$474,824 ...	12.430%	$284,896	$26,777.78
$474,824	$500,000 ...	13.530%	$474,824	$50,385.83
$500,000	and over ...	14.630%	$500,000	$53,792.14

California Withholding Schedules For 2024

California Withholding Schedules for 2024

METHOD B---EXACT CALCULATION METHOD

TABLE 5 - TAX RATE TABLE

SEMI-MONTHLY PAYROLL PERIOD
SINGLE PERSONS, DUAL INCOME MARRIED, OR MARRIED WITH MULTIPLE EMPLOYERS

IF THE TAXABLE INCOME IS... / THE COMPUTED TAX IS...

OVER	BUT NOT OVER	OF AMOUNT OVER...		PLUS
$0	$434 ...	1.100%	$0	$0.00
$434	$1,029 ...	2.200%	$434	$4.77
$1,029	$1,623 ...	4.400%	$1,029	$17.86
$1,623	$2,253 ...	6.600%	$1,623	$44.00
$2,253	$2,848 ...	8.800%	$2,253	$85.58
$2,848	$14,547 ...	10.230%	$2,848	$137.94
$14,547	$17,457 ...	11.330%	$14,547	$1,334.75
$17,457	$29,095 ...	12.430%	$17,457	$1,664.45
$29,095	$41,667 ...	13.530%	$29,095	$3,111.05
$41,667	and over ...	14.630%	$41,667	$4,812.04

MARRIED PERSONS

IF THE TAXABLE INCOME IS... / THE COMPUTED TAX IS...

OVER	BUT NOT OVER	OF AMOUNT OVER...		PLUS
$0	$868 ...	1.100%	$0	$0.00
$868	$2,058 ...	2.200%	$868	$9.55
$2,058	$3,246 ...	4.400%	$2,058	$35.73
$3,246	$4,506 ...	6.600%	$3,246	$88.00
$4,506	$5,696 ...	8.800%	$4,506	$171.16
$5,696	$29,094 ...	10.230%	$5,696	$275.88
$29,094	$34,914 ...	11.330%	$29,094	$2,669.50
$34,914	$41,667 ...	12.430%	$34,914	$3,328.91
$41,667	$58,189 ...	13.530%	$41,667	$4,168.31
$58,189	and over ...	14.630%	$58,189	$6,403.74

UNMARRIED/HEAD OF HOUSEHOLD

IF THE TAXABLE INCOME IS... / THE COMPUTED TAX IS...

OVER	BUT NOT OVER	OF AMOUNT OVER...		PLUS
$0	$868 ...	1.100%	$0	$0.00
$868	$2,057 ...	2.200%	$868	$9.55
$2,057	$2,652 ...	4.400%	$2,057	$35.71
$2,652	$3,282 ...	6.600%	$2,652	$61.89
$3,282	$3,877 ...	8.800%	$3,282	$103.47
$3,877	$19,784 ...	10.230%	$3,877	$155.83
$19,784	$23,741 ...	11.330%	$19,784	$1,783.12
$23,741	$39,569 ...	12.430%	$23,741	$2,231.45
$39,569	$41,667 ...	13.530%	$39,569	$4,198.87
$41,667	and over ...	14.630%	$41,667	$4,482.73

MONTHLY PAYROLL PERIOD
SINGLE PERSONS, DUAL INCOME MARRIED, OR MARRIED WITH MULTIPLE EMPLOYERS

IF THE TAXABLE INCOME IS... / THE COMPUTED TAX IS...

OVER	BUT NOT OVER	OF AMOUNT OVER...		PLUS
$0	$868 ...	1.100%	$0	$0.00
$868	$2,058 ...	2.200%	$868	$9.55
$2,058	$3,246 ...	4.400%	$2,058	$35.73
$3,246	$4,506 ...	6.600%	$3,246	$88.00
$4,506	$5,696 ...	8.800%	$4,506	$171.16
$5,696	$29,094 ...	10.230%	$5,696	$275.88
$29,094	$34,914 ...	11.330%	$29,094	$2,669.50
$34,914	$58,190 ...	12.430%	$34,914	$3,328.91
$58,190	$83,334 ...	13.530%	$58,190	$6,222.12
$83,334	and over ...	14.630%	$83,334	$9,624.10

MARRIED PERSONS

IF THE TAXABLE INCOME IS... / THE COMPUTED TAX IS...

OVER	BUT NOT OVER	OF AMOUNT OVER...		PLUS
$0	$1,736 ...	1.100%	$0	$0.00
$1,736	$4,116 ...	2.200%	$1,736	$19.10
$4,116	$6,492 ...	4.400%	$4,116	$71.46
$6,492	$9,012 ...	6.600%	$6,492	$176.00
$9,012	$11,392 ...	8.800%	$9,012	$342.32
$11,392	$58,188 ...	10.230%	$11,392	$551.76
$58,188	$69,828 ...	11.330%	$58,188	$5,338.99
$69,828	$83,334 ...	12.430%	$69,828	$6,657.80
$83,334	$116,378 ...	13.530%	$83,334	$8,336.60
$116,378	and over ...	14.630%	$116,378	$12,807.45

UNMARRIED/HEAD OF HOUSEHOLD

IF THE TAXABLE INCOME IS... / THE COMPUTED TAX IS...

OVER	BUT NOT OVER	OF AMOUNT OVER...		PLUS
$0	$1,736 ...	1.100%	$0	$0.00
$1,736	$4,114 ...	2.200%	$1,736	$19.10
$4,114	$5,304 ...	4.400%	$4,114	$71.42
$5,304	$6,564 ...	6.600%	$5,304	$123.78
$6,564	$7,754 ...	8.800%	$6,564	$206.94
$7,754	$39,568 ...	10.230%	$7,754	$311.66
$39,568	$47,482 ...	11.330%	$39,568	$3,566.23
$47,482	$79,138 ...	12.430%	$47,482	$4,462.89
$79,138	$83,334 ...	13.530%	$79,138	$8,397.73
$83,334	and over ...	14.630%	$83,334	$8,965.45

California Withholding Schedules For 2024

California Withholding Schedules for 2024

METHOD B---EXACT CALCULATION METHOD

TABLE 5 - TAX RATE TABLE

WEEKLY PAYROLL PERIOD

SINGLE PERSONS, DUAL INCOME MARRIED,
OR MARRIED WITH MULTIPLE EMPLOYERS

IF THE TAXABLE INCOME IS...		THE COMPUTED TAX IS...		
OVER	BUT NOT OVER	OF AMOUNT OVER...		PLUS
$0	$200 ...	1.100%	$0	$0.00
$200	$475 ...	2.200%	$200	$2.20
$475	$749 ...	4.400%	$475	$8.25
$749	$1,040 ...	6.600%	$749	$20.31
$1,040	$1,314 ...	8.800%	$1,040	$39.52
$1,314	$6,714 ...	10.230%	$1,314	$63.63
$6,714	$8,057 ...	11.330%	$6,714	$616.05
$8,057	$13,428 ...	12.430%	$8,057	$768.21
$13,428	$19,231 ...	13.530%	$13,428	$1,435.83
$19,231	and over ...	14.630%	$19,231	$2,220.98

MARRIED PERSONS

IF THE TAXABLE INCOME IS...		THE COMPUTED TAX IS...		
OVER	BUT NOT OVER	OF AMOUNT OVER...		PLUS
$0	$400 ...	1.100%	$0	$0.00
$400	$950 ...	2.200%	$400	$4.40
$950	$1,498 ...	4.400%	$950	$16.50
$1,498	$2,080 ...	6.600%	$1,498	$40.61
$2,080	$2,628 ...	8.800%	$2,080	$79.02
$2,628	$13,428 ...	10.230%	$2,628	$127.24
$13,428	$16,114 ...	11.330%	$13,428	$1,232.08
$16,114	$19,231 ...	12.430%	$16,114	$1,536.40
$19,231	$26,857 ...	13.530%	$19,231	$1,923.84
$26,857	and over ...	14.630%	$26,857	$2,955.64

UNMARRIED/HEAD OF HOUSEHOLD

IF THE TAXABLE INCOME IS...		THE COMPUTED TAX IS...		
OVER	BUT NOT OVER	OF AMOUNT OVER...		PLUS
$0	$401 ...	1.100%	$0	$0.00
$401	$949 ...	2.200%	$401	$4.41
$949	$1,224 ...	4.400%	$949	$16.47
$1,224	$1,515 ...	6.600%	$1,224	$28.57
$1,515	$1,789 ...	8.800%	$1,515	$47.78
$1,789	$9,131 ...	10.230%	$1,789	$71.89
$9,131	$10,958 ...	11.330%	$9,131	$822.98
$10,958	$18,262 ...	12.430%	$10,958	$1,029.98
$18,262	$19,231 ...	13.530%	$18,262	$1,937.87
$19,231	and over ...	14.630%	$19,231	$2,068.98

BIWEEKLY PAYROLL PERIOD

SINGLE PERSONS, DUAL INCOME MARRIED,
OR MARRIED WITH MULTIPLE EMPLOYERS

IF THE TAXABLE INCOME IS...		THE COMPUTED TAX IS...		
OVER	BUT NOT OVER	OF AMOUNT OVER...		PLUS
$0	$400 ...	1.100%	$0	$0.00
$400	$950 ...	2.200%	$400	$4.40
$950	$1,498 ...	4.400%	$950	$16.50
$1,498	$2,080 ...	6.600%	$1,498	$40.61
$2,080	$2,628 ...	8.800%	$2,080	$79.02
$2,628	$13,428 ...	10.230%	$2,628	$127.24
$13,428	$16,114 ...	11.330%	$13,428	$1,232.08
$16,114	$26,856 ...	12.430%	$16,114	$1,536.40
$26,856	$38,462 ...	13.530%	$26,856	$2,871.63
$38,462	and over ...	14.630%	$38,462	$4,441.92

MARRIED PERSONS

IF THE TAXABLE INCOME IS...		THE COMPUTED TAX IS...		
OVER	BUT NOT OVER	OF AMOUNT OVER...		PLUS
$0	$800 ...	1.100%	$0	$0.00
$800	$1,900 ...	2.200%	$800	$8.80
$1,900	$2,996 ...	4.400%	$1,900	$33.00
$2,996	$4,160 ...	6.600%	$2,996	$81.22
$4,160	$5,256 ...	8.800%	$4,160	$158.04
$5,256	$26,856 ...	10.230%	$5,256	$254.49
$26,856	$32,228 ...	11.330%	$26,856	$2,464.17
$32,228	$38,462 ...	12.430%	$32,228	$3,072.82
$38,462	$53,714 ...	13.530%	$38,462	$3,847.71
$53,714	and over ...	14.630%	$53,714	$5,911.31

UNMARRIED/HEAD OF HOUSEHOLD

IF THE TAXABLE INCOME IS...		THE COMPUTED TAX IS...		
OVER	BUT NOT OVER	OF AMOUNT OVER...		PLUS
$0	$802 ...	1.100%	$0	$0.00
$802	$1,898 ...	2.200%	$802	$8.82
$1,898	$2,448 ...	4.400%	$1,898	$32.93
$2,448	$3,030 ...	6.600%	$2,448	$57.13
$3,030	$3,578 ...	8.800%	$3,030	$95.54
$3,578	$18,262 ...	10.230%	$3,578	$143.76
$18,262	$21,916 ...	11.330%	$18,262	$1,645.93
$21,916	$36,524 ...	12.430%	$21,916	$2,059.93
$36,524	$38,462 ...	13.530%	$36,524	$3,875.70
$38,462	and over ...	14.630%	$38,462	$4,137.91

California Withholding Schedules For 2024

E-file and E-pay Mandate

All employers are required to electronically submit their employment tax returns, wage reports, and payroll tax deposits to the EDD.

Benefits of Electronic Filing and Payment

- Increases data accuracy.

- Protects data through encryption.

- Reduces paper and mailing cost.

- Eliminates lost mail.

Penalty	
Paper Submittal	**Penalty**
Tax Return: • *Quarterly Contribution Return and Report of Wages* (DE 9) • *Employer of Household Worker(s) Annual Payroll Tax Return* (DE 3HW) • *Quarterly Contribution Return* (DE 3D)	$50 per return
Wage Report: • *Quarterly Contribution Return and Report of Wages (Continuation)* (DE 9C) • *Employer of Household Worker(s) Quarterly Report of Wages and Withholdings* (DE 3BHW)	$20 per wage item
Payroll Tax Deposit: • *Payroll Tax Deposit* (DE 88)	15% of amount due

Note: Filing a paper tax return to indicate that no wages were paid will result in a noncompliance penalty of $50.

Waiver

Employers may request a waiver from the mandate due to lack of automation, severe economic hardship, current exemption from the federal government, or other good cause. Mandate waiver requests cannot be filed retroactively. You will receive an approval or denial letter from the EDD by mail. The approval letter will indicate the approval period. Upon the expiration of the approval period, you must start to electronically file and pay. If you are still unable to electronically file and pay, you must submit a new waiver request to avoid any non-compliance penalties.

For more information, visit E-file and E-pay Mandate for Employers (edd.ca.gov/en/Payroll_Taxes/E-file_and_E-pay_Mandate_for_Employers). You can download the *E-file and E-pay Mandate Waiver Request* (DE 1245W) (PDF) (edd.ca.gov/pdf_pub_ctr/de1245w.pdf) or contact the Taxpayer Assistance Center at 1-888-745-3886.

Enroll in e-Services for Business
(edd.ca.gov/eServices)
to help you meet the requirements
of the e-file and e-pay mandate.
Fast, easy, and secure!

e-Services for Business

e-Services for Business allows employers, employer representatives, and payroll agents to manage employer payroll tax accounts online at no cost. With a simple one-time enrollment, e-Services for Business can be used to electronically submit employment tax returns, wage reports, and payments 24 hours a day, 7 days a week.*

Enroll in e-Services for Business
(edd.ca.gov/eServices).
Fast, easy, and secure!

Features:

- Register, close, or re-open an employer payroll tax account.
- File, adjust, and print tax returns and wage reports.
- Make payments.
- Report changes to your business.
- Protest Unemployment Insurance (UI) benefit charges or UI rates.
- Authorize a power of attorney.
- View notices and letters.
- Report new employees or independent contractors.
- Request a transfer of a reserve account.

Benefits:

- Fulfills the e-file and e-pay mandate for employers.
- No cost to enroll and use.
- Provides confirmation when your return, report, or payment is received.
- Saves time by saving basic account information for future transactions.
- Reduces paper and mailing cost.

* The *Report of New Employee(s)* (DE 34) and *Report of Independent Contractor(s)* (DE 542) may be filed from 5 a.m. to 12 midnight, Pacific time, 7 days a week. All other services may be accessed 24 hours a day, 7 days a week.

Additional e-Services for Business Information	
Tutorials on how to:	**Answers to frequently asked questions about:**
<ul><li>Create a username and password.</li><li>Register for an employer payroll tax account number.</li><li>File a tax return or wage report.</li><li>Make a payroll tax deposit.</li><li>And more.</li></ul> Visit e-Services for Business Tutorials (edd.ca.gov/en/payroll_taxes/ e-Services_for_Business_tutorials.htm) for more!	<ul><li>Accessing an employer payroll tax account.</li><li>Registering, closing, or reopening an account.</li><li>Filing forms and making payments.</li><li>Filing benefit charge and rate protests.</li><li>And more.</li></ul> Frequently Asked Questions (edd.ca.gov/en/payroll_taxes/ FAQ_-_e-Services_for_Business.htm).

Express Pay

Employers and employer representatives or payroll agents can make electronic tax payments without having to register with the EDD. Just enter an employer payroll tax account number or letter ID and payment information to submit a payroll tax deposit or account payment online. Visit File and Pay Options (edd.ca.gov/Payroll_Taxes/File_and_Pay.htm) to make a payment today.

e-Services for Business Tutorials and User Guide

The EDD has created tutorials (edd.ca.gov/payroll_taxes/e-Services_for_Business_tutorials.htm) so employers and employer representatives or payroll agents can become familiar with e-Services for Business.

The *e-Services for Business User Guide* (DE 160) (PDF) (edd.ca.gov/pdf_pub_ctr/de160.pdf) provides detailed step-by-step instructions on how to complete common tasks within e-Services for Business such as, creating a username and password, filing a tax return and wage report, making a payroll tax deposit, and more.

Frequently Asked Questions

For answers to frequently asked questions (FAQs) regarding our electronic services, such as filing returns and reports, making payments, bulk transfer options, and more, visit FAQs for e-Services for Business (edd.ca.gov/Payroll_Taxes/FAQ_-_e-Services_for_Business.htm).

For more information regarding e-Services for Business (edd.ca.gov/eServices) contact the Taxpayer Assistance Center at 1-888-745-3886.

Go Paperless!
You can view or download this guide at California Employer Guides
(edd.ca.gov/en/Payroll_Taxes/Employers_Guides).

For the latest tax news and employer resources, visit
California Employer News and Updates
(edd.ca.gov/payroll_taxes/employer-news.htm).

Subscribe to the EDD no-cost email subscription services
(edd.ca.gov/about_edd/get_email_notices.htm).

Required Forms

Under California law, you are required to report specific information periodically or upon notification or request. Timely filing of the required forms will avoid penalty and interest charges. In addition, it will enable the Employment Development Department (EDD) to pay Unemployment Insurance (UI), Disability Insurance (DI), and Paid Family Leave (PFL) benefits. Timely filing also assists the California Department of Child Support Services and the Department of Justice in the collection of delinquent child support obligations. Refer to page 49 for the information on the e-file and e-pay mandate and related noncompliance penalties.

Required reporting forms are:

- *Report of New Employee(s) (DE 34)*

- *Report of Independent Contractor(s) (DE 542)*

- *Payroll Tax Deposit (DE 88)*

- *Quarterly Contribution Return and Report of Wages (DE 9)*

- *Quarterly Contribution Return and Report of Wages (Continuation) (DE 9C)*

Go Paperless!
You can view or download this guide at California Employer Guides
(edd.ca.gov/en/Payroll_Taxes/Employers_Guides).

For the latest tax news and employer resources, visit
California Employer News and Updates
(edd.ca.gov/payroll_taxes/employer-news.htm).

Subscribe to the EDD no-cost email subscription services
(edd.ca.gov/about_edd/get_email_notices.htm).

Report of New Employee(s) (DE 34)

Overview

All employers are required by law to report all newly hired or rehired employees to the New Employee Registry (NER) within 20 days of their start-of-work date, which is the first day services were performed for wages.

- **Newly Hired** employees are those individuals who have not previously been included on your payroll.

- **Rehired** employees are those individuals who were previously included on your payroll, left your employment, and were rehired after a separation of at least 60 consecutive days.

If you acquire an ongoing business and employ any of the former employees, they are considered new hires, and you should report them to the EDD's NER. The NER assists California's Department of Child Support Services and Department of Justice in locating parents to collect delinquent child support payments. Employers must also report the actual start-of-work date, not the date hired, for each newly hired or rehired employee so that the NER data can be cross-matched to the UI benefit payment file. This will result in the early detection and prevention of UI benefit overpayments.

Options for Reporting New or Rehired Employees:

1. File through e-Services for Business (edd.ca.gov/eServices).
2. Download and mail or fax the *Report of New Employee(s) (DE 34) (PDF)* (edd.ca.gov/pdf_pub_ctr/de34.pdf).
3. Order the DE 34 at Online Forms and Publications (forms.edd.ca.gov/forms).

You must report all newly hired or rehired employees **within 20 days** of the start-of-work date. If an employee returns to work after a layoff or leave of absence and is required to complete a new IRS *Employee's Withholding Certificate* Form W-4 and state *Employee Withholding Allowance Certificate* (DE 4), you must report the employee as a new hire. If the returning employee had been separated or removed from payroll records for at least 60 consecutive days, then you need to report the employee as a rehire.

Include the following information when reporting new or rehired employees:

Employer Information	Employee Information
• EDD eight-digit employer payroll tax account number. • Federal Employer Identification Number (FEIN). • Business name. • Business address. • Contact person and phone number.	• First name, middle initial, and last name. • Social Security number. • Home address. • Start-of-work date.

Refer to sample DE 34 form on page 54.

Filing an Informal Report

If you are not able to obtain a DE 34 by the due date, file an informal report or a copy of the employee's DE 4 to avoid penalty and interest charges. Your informal report must include all the information listed in the table above.

Mail or fax your new employee information to:

Employment Development Department
Document Management Group, MIC 96
PO Box 997016
West Sacramento, CA 95799-7016

Fax: 1-916-319-4400

Employers who hire employees in more than one state may elect to electronically report all newly hired employees to one state in which they have employees. Multistate employers who choose to file in one state must notify the Office of Child Support Enforcement (acf.hhs.gov/programs/css/resource/ocse-multistate-employer-registration-contacts).

You can file online using e-Services for Business (edd.ca.gov/eServices). It's fast, easy, and secure. **If You File Electronically, Do Not File a Paper DE 34.**

For additional information on new employee electronic filing, refer to the *Electronic Filing Guide for the New Employee Registry Program (DE 340) (PDF)* (edd.ca.gov/pdf_pub_ctr/de340.pdf) or the California New Employee Registry FAQs (edd.ca.gov/payroll_taxes/faq_-_california_new_employee_registry.htm), or contact the Taxpayer Assistance Center at 1-888-745-3886.

REPORT OF NEW EMPLOYEE(S)

EDD Employment Development Department
State of California

NOTE: *Failure to provide all of the information below may result in this form being rejected and/or a penalty being assessed.*

00340600

DATE	CA EMPLOYER ACCOUNT NUMBER	BRANCH CODE	FEDERAL ID NUMBER
030423 D Y Y	00000000		xxxxxxxxx

BUSINESS NAME	CONTACT PERSON	PHONE NUMBER
EMPLOYER CITY STORE	JANE SMITH	123-555-7789

ADDRESS	STREET	CITY	STATE	ZIP CODE
PO BOX 12345		ANYTOWN CA	12345	

EMPLOYEE FIRST NAME	MI	EMPLOYEE LAST NAME
	E	MILLER

SOCIAL SECURITY NUMBER · STREET NUMBER · STREET NAME: CEDAR STREET · UNIT/APT

CITY	STATE	ZIP CODE	START-OF-WORK DATE
	CA	12345	022523 D Y Y

File this form online through e-Services for Business (edd.ca.gov/eServices).

EMPLOYEE FIRST NAME	MI	EMPLOYEE LAST NAME

SOCIAL SECURITY NUMBER · STREET NUMBER · STREET NAME · UNIT/APT

CITY	STATE	ZIP CODE	START-OF-WORK DATE
			M M D D Y Y

EMPLOYEE FIRST NAME	MI	EMPLOYEE LAST NAME

SOCIAL SECURITY NUMBER · STREET NUMBER · STREET NAME · UNIT/APT

CITY	STATE	ZIP CODE	START-OF-WORK DATE
			M M D D Y Y

EMPLOYEE FIRST NAME	MI	EMPLOYEE LAST NAME

SOCIAL SECURITY NUMBER · STREET NUMBER · STREET NAME · UNIT/APT

CITY	STATE	ZIP CODE	START-OF-WORK DATE
			M M D D Y Y

EMPLOYEE FIRST NAME	MI	EMPLOYEE LAST NAME

SOCIAL SECURITY NUMBER · STREET NUMBER · STREET NAME · UNIT/APT

CITY	STATE	ZIP CODE	START-OF-WORK DATE
			M M D D Y Y

EMPLOYEE FIRST NAME	MI	EMPLOYEE LAST NAME

SOCIAL SECURITY NUMBER · STREET NUMBER · STREET NAME · UNIT/APT

CITY	STATE	ZIP CODE	START-OF-WORK DATE
			M M D D Y Y

Required Forms

DE 34 Rev. 10 (3-17) **(INTERNET)**   Page 1 of 2   MAIL TO: Employment Development Department / PO Box 997016, MIC 96 West Sacramento, CA 95799-7016 or fax to 916-319-4400   CU

Report of Independent Contractor(s) (DE 542)

Overview

Any business or government entity that is required to file the federal Forms 1099-MISC or 1099-NEC for personal services performed must also report specific information to the Employment Development Department (EDD) regarding any independent contractor providing services to you or your business. The Independent Contractor Reporting (ICR) information assists California's Department of Child Support Services and Department of Justice in locating parents for the purpose of collecting delinquent child support payments. An independent contractor is an individual who is not an employee under the ABC test or statutory employee of a business or government entity for California purposes and who receives compensation for, or executes a contract for, services performed for a business and/or government entity, either in or outside of California.

Options for Reporting Independent Contractors:

1. File through e-Services for Business (edd.ca.gov/eServices).
2. Download and mail or fax the *Report of Independent Contractor(s) (DE 542) (PDF)* (edd.ca.gov/pdf_pub_ctr/de542.pdf).
3. Order the DE 542 at Online Forms and Publications (edd.ca.gov/forms).

Important Due Dates: Independent contractor information must be reported to the EDD within 20 days of either making payments totaling $600 or more or entering into a contract for $600 or more with an independent contractor in any calendar year, whichever occurs first. This is in addition to your requirement to report the total annual payments to the Internal Revenue Service on the Forms 1099-MISC or 1099-NEC after the close of the calendar year.

Include the following information when reporting independent contractors:

Business or Government Entity (Service-Recipient) Information	Independent Contractor (Service-Provider) Information
<ul><li>Federal Employer Identification Number (FEIN).</li><li>EDD eight-digit employer payroll tax account number (if applicable).</li><li>Social Security number (if no FEIN number or eight-digit EDD employer payroll tax account number).</li><li>Business or government entity name, address, and phone number.</li><li>Contact person.</li></ul>	<ul><li>First name, middle initial, and last name (do not use company name).</li><li>Social Security number (do not use FEIN).</li><li>Address.</li><li>Start date of contract.</li><li>Amount of contract (including cents).</li><li>Contract expiration date or check box if the contract is ongoing.</li></ul>

Refer to sample DE 542 on page 56.

Filing an Informal Report

If you are not able to obtain a DE 542 by the due date, you may file an informal report to avoid penalty and interest charges. Your informal report must include all the information listed in the table above.

Mail or fax your independent contractor information to:

Employment Development Department
Document Management Group, MIC 96
PO Box 997350
Sacramento, CA 95899-7350

Fax: 1-916-319-4410

If you are reporting a large number of independent contractors, we encourage you to send the information electronically. You can file online using e-Services for Business (edd.ca.gov/eServices). **If You File Electronically, Do Not File a Paper DE 542**. For additional information on **ICR electronic filing**, refer to the *Electronic Filing Guide for the Independent Contractor Reporting Program (DE 542M) (PDF)* (edd.ca.gov/pdf_pub_ctr/de542m.pdf), the ICR FAQs (edd.ca.gov/siteassets/files/pdf_pub_ctr/de542faq.pdf), and ICR reporting (edd.ca.gov/payroll_taxes/faq_-_california_independent_contractor_reporting.htm), or by contacting the Taxpayer Assistance Center at 1-888-745-3886.

Required Forms

For Illustrative Purposes Only

EDD Employment Development Department
State of California

REPORT OF INDEPENDENT CONTRACTOR(S)
See detailed instructions on reverse side. Please type or print.

05420101

SERVICE-RECIPIENT (BUSINESS OR GOVERNMENT ENTITY):

DATE	FEDERAL ID NUMBER	CA EMPLOYER ACCOUNT NUMBER	SOCIAL SECURITY NUMBER
031423	XXXXXXXXX	00000000	XXXXXXXX

SERVICE-RECIPIENT NAME / BUSINESS NAME	CONTACT PERSON
EMPLOYER CITY STORE	JANE SMITH

ADDRE...

File this form online through e-Services for Business (edd.ca.gov/eServices).

PHONE NUMBER: 123 555-7899

STATE: CA   ZIP CODE: 12345

SERVICE-PROVIDER (INDEPENDENT CONTRACTOR):

FIRST NAME	MI	LAST NAME
HENRY	A	KENNEDY

SOCIAL SECURITY NUMBER	STREET NUMBER	STREET NAME	UNIT/APT
000000000	2954	HILLCREST DRIVE	

CITY	STATE	ZIP CODE
ANYCITY	CA	12345

START DATE OF CONTRACT	AMOUNT OF CONTRACT	CONTRACT EXPIRATION DATE	CHECK HERE IF CONTRACT IS ONGOING
030423	1000.00	063023	
M M D D Y Y		M M D D Y Y	

FIRST NAME	MI	LAST NAME

SOCIAL SECURITY NUMBER	STREET NUMBER	STREET NAME	UNIT/APT

CITY	STATE	ZIP CODE

START DATE OF CONTRACT	AMOUNT OF CONTRACT	CONTRACT EXPIRATION DATE	CHECK HERE IF CONTRACT IS ONGOING
M M D D Y Y		M M D D Y Y	

FIRST NAME	MI	LAST NAME

SOCIAL SECURITY NUMBER	STREET NUMBER	STREET NAME	UNIT/APT

CITY	STATE	ZIP CODE

START DATE OF CONTRACT	AMOUNT OF CONTRACT	CONTRACT EXPIRATION DATE	CHECK HERE IF CONTRACT IS ONGOING
M M D D Y Y		M M D D Y Y	

MAIL TO: Employment Development Department • PO Box 997350, MIC 96 • Sacramento, CA 95899-7350
or Fax to 916-319-4410

DE 542 Rev. 9 (6-17) **(INTERNET)**   **Page 1 of 2**

Payroll Tax Deposit (DE 88)

Overview

The *Payroll Tax Deposit* (DE 88) is used to report and pay Unemployment Insurance (UI) tax, Employment Training Tax (ETT), State Disability Insurance (SDI) tax withholding, and Personal Income Tax (PIT) withholding to the Employment Development Department (EDD). Employers can enroll and use e-Services for Business to make deposits.

 e-Services for Business. Fast, easy and secure!

Electronic Filing with e-Services for Business:

- All employers must electronically submit payroll tax deposits. Refer to page 49 for additional information on the e-file and e-pay mandate and related noncompliance penalties.
- Fulfills the e-file and e-pay mandate.
- Fast, easy, and secure way to manage your payroll taxes online.
- Available 24 hours a day, 7 days a week.
- Employer representatives or payroll agents can manage their clients' payroll tax accounts by enrolling in e-Services for Business as a Representative or Agent.
- For additional e-Services for Business features, refer to page 50.

Enroll and file through e-Services for Business (edd.ca.gov/eServices) today.

Important Due Dates:

- If you do not withhold PIT or if accumulated PIT withholdings are less than $350, taxes (UI, ETT, SDI, and PIT) are due each quarter on January 1, April 1, July 1, and October 1.
- If PIT withholdings are $350 or more, SDI and PIT may need to be deposited more often. Refer to page 6 for the California Deposit Requirements table.

Note: A penalty of 15 percent plus interest will be charged on late payroll ta x payments. Your UI, ETT, and SDI tax rates are available on your e-Services for Business account.

For additional assistance, contact the Taxpayer Assistance Center at 1-888-745-3886. If outside of the U.S. or Canada, call 1-916-464-3502.

Go Paperless!
You can view or download this guide at California Employer Guides (edd.ca.gov/en/Payroll_Taxes/Employers_Guides).

Withholding Deposits

All employers must electronically submit payroll tax deposits to the EDD. Refer to page 49 for information on the e-file and e-pay mandate and related noncompliance penalties. Employers can enroll and use e-Services for Business (edd.ca.gov/eServices) to submit a *Payroll Tax Deposit* (DE 88) electronically. Although employer contributions of Unemployment Insurance (UI) and Employment Training Tax (ETT) are due quarterly, **withholdings from employee wages for State Disability Insurance (SDI) and Personal Income Tax (PIT) may need to be deposited more often**. The SDI and PIT deposit due dates are based on each employer's federal deposit schedule or requirement and the amount of accumulated PIT the employer has withheld. Details are provided below and in the table on page 59. For information on federal deposit schedules, download the IRS Employer's Tax Guide (Publication 15, Circular E) at IRS (irs.gov) or contact the IRS at 1-800-829-3676.

A penalty of 15 percent plus interest will be charged on late payroll tax payments.

California Deposit Requirements

California Deposit Schedule	Requirement Definition
Next-Day	You are required to make next-day SDI and PIT deposits if you are required to make federal next-day deposits and you accumulate more than $500* in California PIT during one or more payroll periods. **If you accumulate $350 to $500* in PIT during one or more pay periods, refer to monthly requirements below.**
	The next-day deposit schedule requires deposits to be made by the next business day. Business days do not include Saturdays, Sundays, or federal holidays.
Semi-weekly	You are required to make semi-weekly SDI and PIT deposits if you are required to make federal semi-weekly deposits and you accumulate more than $500* in California PIT during one or more payroll periods. **If you accumulate $350 to $500* in PIT during one or more pay periods, refer to monthly requirements below.**
	The semi-weekly deposit schedule requires deposits for paydays on Wednesday, Thursday, and Friday to be made by the following Wednesday. For paydays on Saturday, Sunday, Monday, or Tuesday, deposits must be made by the following Friday.
	Semi-weekly depositors always have three business days after the end of the semi-weekly period to make a deposit. If any of the three business days after the end of the semi-weekly period is a legal holiday, you will have an additional business day to make your deposit.
Monthly	You are required to make monthly SDI and PIT deposits if you are required to make federal annual, quarterly, or monthly deposits and you accumulate $350 or more in California PIT during one or more months of a quarter.
	Monthly deposits are due by the 15th day of the following month. If the 15th is a Saturday, Sunday, or federal holiday, the last timely date would be the next business day.
	You are required to make monthly SDI and PIT deposits if you are required to make federal semi-weekly or next-day deposits **and you accumulate $350 to $500* in California PIT during one or more months of a quarter.**
Quarterly	**Quarterly tax payments are due and delinquent on the same dates as the *Quarterly Contribution Return and Report of Wages (Continuation)* (DE 9C)**. Refer to the monthly deposit schedule if you are a quarterly depositor but accumulate $350 or more in California PIT during one or more months of the quarter.
	Employer contributions for UI and ETT are due quarterly. However, they may be submitted more often with any required SDI and PIT deposits.

*California PIT deposit threshold may be adjusted annually. Refer to the California Deposit Requirements on page 6.

Required Forms

Due Dates for Quarterly Tax Deposits

Using Electronic Funds Transfer

Electronic Funds Transfer (EFT) transactions, regardless of the method of transmission, e-Services for Business, vendor, or Federal and State Employment Taxes program, for quarterly Unemployment Insurance (UI) tax, Employment Training Tax (ETT), State Disability Insurance (SDI) Tax, and Personal Income Tax (PIT) withholding payments must settle in the state's bank account on or before the timely settlement date. Refer to the last column in the table below for specific settlement dates.

2024 Quarterly Payment Table

Reporting Period	Taxes Due	Last Timely Date (initiate on or before)	Timely Settlement Date
January, February, March	April 1, 2024	April 30, 2024	May 1, 2024
April, May, June	July 1, 2024	July 31, 2024	August 1, 2024
July, August, September	October 1, 2024	October 31, 2024	November 1, 2024
October, November, December	January 1, 2025	January 31, 2025	February 3, 2025

To ensure timely settlement of your electronic payments, please note:

- EFT Automated Clearing House (ACH) debit transactions must be completed before 3 p.m., Pacific time, on or before the last timely date to ensure a timely settlement date.

- The EFT ACH credit transactions are processed based on individual bank requirements. Ask your bank what day you should report your payment to ensure a timely settlement date.

Using a *Payroll Tax Deposit* (DE 88) Coupon

All employers must electronically submit payroll tax deposits to the EDD. Refer to page 49 for additional information on the e-file and e-pay mandate and related noncompliance penalties. Employers who have an approved e-file and e-pay mandate waiver can mail the tax payments with a DE 88 to the EDD. **A penalty of 15 percent plus interest will be charged on late payroll tax payments.** The filing due dates and delinquency dates for 2024 quarterly payroll tax deposits are:

Reporting Period	Filing Due Date	Delinquent if Not Paid By
January, February, March	April 1, 2024	April 30, 2024
April, May, June	July 1, 2024	July 31, 2024
July, August, September	October 1, 2024	October 31, 2024
October, November, December	January 1, 2025	January 31, 2025

Late Deposit, Penalty, and Interest

When tax payments are remitted electronically, the settlement date is used to determine timeliness. When your tax payments are mailed to the EDD, the postmark date is used to determine timeliness. If the last timely filing date falls on a Saturday, Sunday, or federal holiday, the next business day is the last timely date. **A penalty of 15 percent plus interest will be charged on late payroll tax payments.** The interest rate is reestablished every six months. Refer to the Interest Rate on Overdue Taxes (edd.ca.gov/payroll_taxes/interest_rate.htm).

Note: If you do not make timely payments, you will receive a *Statement of Account* (DE 2176) that provides details of the delinquent balance due. If the delinquency is not paid, a State Tax Lien may be issued. If a State Tax Lien is issued, it will be recorded at the county recorder's office and the Secretary of State. Tax lien information is a matter of public record after it is recorded.

Penalty for Failure to Deposit Payroll Taxes

Employers are required to withhold payroll taxes and send them to the EDD. Any person or employer who fails to do this, even by mistake, can be charged with a misdemeanor. If convicted, the person or employer can be fined up to $1,000 or sentenced to jail for up to one year, or both, at the discretion of the court.

Correcting Previously Submitted *Payroll Tax Deposit* (DE 88)

Payroll tax deposits can be corrected online through e-Services for Business (edd.ca.gov/eServices) even if the deposit was made using another electronic payment method or a paper DE 88 coupon.

Note: All employers must electronically submit payroll tax deposits to the EDD. Refer to page 49 for additional information on the e-file and e-pay mandate and related noncompliance penalties.

The following table clarifies when and how to notify the EDD of adjustments to payroll tax deposits.

Type of Adjustment	How to Make Adjustment
Overpaid UI, ETT, SDI, or PIT on a DE 88 prior to filing your DE 9 for the quarter.	On the next DE 88 for the same calendar quarter, reduce the amount of taxers due by the amount of the overpayment. Do not show credits (negative amounts) on the DE 88. If you cannot reduce the overpayment on your next deposit within the quarter, claim the amount overpaid in the **Total Taxes Due or Overpaid** field of your DE 9 when you file your return for the quarter.
Underpaid UI, ETT, SDI, or PIT **prior to filing your DE 9 for the quarter**.	Submit a DE 88 to pay the amount due, including penalty and interest. To find current rates or to calculate interests visit Interest Rate on Overdue Taxes (edd.ca.gov/en/Payroll_Taxes/Interest_Rate). Indicate the payroll date on the DE 88. The penalty amount is 15% of the portion of the payment that is late.
Allocated the wrong amounts to specific funds on a DE 88 prior to filing the DE 9 for the quarter.	**Do Not Adjust:** The EDD will make the necessary adjustments at the end of the quarter when you file your DE 9.
Underpaid UI, ETT, SDI, or PIT and your **DE 9 was previously filed with correct information.**	Submit a **DE 88** for the additional amount due for the quarter, including any penalty and interest, or pay the balance due when you receive a *Statement of Account* (DE 2176) in the mail. To find current rates or to calculate interests visit Interest Rate on Overdue Taxes (edd.ca.gov/en/Payroll_Taxes/Interest_Rate). The penalty amount is 15% of the portion of the payment that is late.

Note: Overwithheld SDI or California PIT must be credited or refunded to your employee before you can take a credit or receive a refund from the EDD. You should obtain a receipt from the employee whenever a credit adjustment or refund of overwithheld tax is made.

Refer to How to Correct Prior Reports, Returns, or Deposits (edd.ca.gov/en/payroll_taxes/how_to_correct_prior_reports_or_deposits) or page 68 if adjustments are needed to the DE 9 or DE 9C.

Required Forms

Correcting PIT Withheld

Type of Adjustment	How to Make Adjustment
Overwithheld PIT and: • DE 9 was filed. • DE 9C was filed. • **Wage and Tax Statement (Form W-2) was issued to the employees.**	The employee will receive a credit for the PIT withholding when filing a California state income tax return with the Franchise Tax Board (FTB). • **Do not** refund PIT withholding to the employee. • **Do not** change the California PIT withholding amount shown on the employee(s) Form W-2. • **Do not** file a claim for refund with the EDD.
Overwithheld or Underwithheld PIT • DE 9 was filed. • DE 9C was filed. • **Prior to issuing Form W-2 to the employees.**	Upon receiving written permission from an employee, you are authorized to adjust any over or underwithholding of California PIT from the employee. You should obtain a receipt from the employee whenever the overwithheld PIT is credited or refunded to the employee. Refer to How to Correct Prior Reports, Returns, or Deposits (edd.ca.gov/en/payroll_taxes/how_to_correct_prior_reports_or_deposits) or page 68 for instructions on how to request an adjustment to the DE 9 and/or DE 9C.
Overwithheld or Underwithheld PIT • DE 9 was filed. • DE 9C was filed. • **Form W-2 was issued to the employees with the wrong amounts.**	You must issue an IRS *Corrected Wage and Tax Statement* (Form W-2C) to the employee. Do not send the state copy of the IRS Form W-2C to the EDD or the FTB.

When **written permission** is obtained from an employee, you are authorized to adjust any overwithheld or underwithheld California PIT from the employee if the adjustment is made within the same calendar year and before the IRS Form W-2 is issued.

Overwithheld SDI or California PIT must be credited or refunded to your employee before you can take a credit or receive a refund from the EDD.

Note: A claim for refund must be filed within 3 years of the last timely date of the quarter being adjusted, or within 6 months after an assessment becomes final, or within 60 days from the date of the overpayment, whichever date occurs later.

Go Paperless!
You can view or download this guide at California Employer Guides
(edd.ca.gov/en/Payroll_Taxes/Employers_Guides).

Quarterly Contribution Return and Report of Wages (DE 9)

Overview

Employers use the *Quarterly Contribution Return and Report of Wages* (DE 9) to reconcile payroll tax payments and total subject wages reported for the quarter. You must electronically file a DE 9 and a *Quarterly Contribution Return and Report of Wages (Continuation)* (DE 9C) each quarter. As an active employer, you must file a DE 9 each quarter even if you paid no wages during the quarter. Your DE 9 should indicate that no wages were paid for the quarter. If you no longer have employees or you are no longer in business, refer to page 70 for filing instructions. Effective January 1, 2019, filing a paper return to indicate that no wages were paid will result in a noncompliance penalty of $50. If you need to report wages after your account has been inactivated or ceased, you must reactivate the account and file the return and wage report electronically.

2024 Due Dates for the *Quarterly Contribution Return and Report of Wages* (DE 9)

Report Covering	Due Date	Delinquent if Not Filed By
January, February, March	April 1, 2024	April 30, 2024
April, May, June	July 1, 2024	July 31, 2024
July, August, September	October 1, 2024	October 31, 2024
October, November, December	January 1, 2025	January 31, 2025

Penalty and interest will be charged on late reports. If the **Delinquent if Not Filed By** date falls on a Saturday, Sunday, or legal holiday, the **Delinquent if Not Filed By** date is extended to the next business day.

Note: For reporting purposes, wages are taxable when paid, when constructively paid, or when an employee receives payment other than cash.

Important: All employers must electronically submit employment tax returns, wage reports, and payroll tax deposits to the EDD. Refer to page 49 for additional information on the e-file and e-pay mandate and related noncompliance penalties.

- If your reports are filed late or you do not make timely payments, you will receive a *Statement of Account* (DE 2176) that provides details of the delinquent balance due. If the delinquency is not paid, a State Tax Lien may be issued. If a State Tax Lien is issued, it will be recorded at the county recorder's office and the Secretary of State. A Notice of State Tax Lien information is a matter of public record after it is recorded.

- **A penalty of $50 plus interest** will be charged for filing a paper tax return. For more information, visit E-file and E-pay Mandate for Employers (edd.ca.gov/EfileMandate) or refer to page 49.

Correcting a Previously Filed DE 9

If you made an error on a DE 9, you can make a correction as follows:

Online

Log in to e-Services for Business (edd.ca.gov/eServices) and access the previously filed DE 9 you want to correct. For step-by-step instructions:
- Refer to How to Correct Prior Reports, Returns, or Deposits (edd.ca.gov/en/payroll_taxes/how_to_correct_prior_reports_or_deposits).
- Access the *e-Services for Business User Guide* (DE160) (PDF) (edd.ca.gov/pdf_pub_ctr/de160.pdf).
- View the e-Services for Business Tutorials (edd.ca.gov/en/payroll_taxes/e-Services_for_Business_Tutorials).

Paper

Complete and mail the *Quarterly Contribution and Wage Adjustment Form* (DE 9ADJ). Refer to pages 65 and 66 for additional information and a sample DE 9ADJ form.

Quarterly Contribution Return and Report of Wages (Continuation) (DE 9C)

Overview

Employers use the *Quarterly Contribution Return and Report of Wages (Continuation)* (DE 9C) to report employee wages subject to Unemployment Insurance (UI) tax, Employment Training Tax (ETT), State Disability Insurance (SDI) tax, and to report Personal Income Tax (PIT) wages and PIT withheld. As an active employer, you must electronically file a DE 9C each quarter even if you paid no wages during the quarter indicating you do not have the payroll to report. If you no longer have employees or are no longer in business, refer to page 70 for filing instructions. If you need to report wages after your account has been inactivated or ceased, you must reactivate the account and file the return and wage report electronically.

2024 Due Dates for the DE 9C

Report Covering	Due Date	Delinquent if Not Filed By
January, February, March	April 1, 2024	April 30, 2024
April, May, June	July 1, 2024	July 31, 2024
July, August, September	October 1, 2024	October 31, 2024
October, November, December	January 1, 2025	January 31, 2025

Penalty and interest will be charged on late reports. If the **Delinquent if Not Filed By** date falls on a Saturday, Sunday, or federal holiday, the **Delinquent if Not Filed By** date is extended to the next business day.

Note: For reporting purposes, wages are taxable when paid, when constructively paid, or when an employee receives payment other than cash. If wages are still unpaid at the time the DE 9C is due, wages due to an employee that were not paid within the time required by law should be reported by filing the *Quarterly Contribution and Wage Adjustment Form* (DE 9ADJ) online through e-Services for Business with *Wages Legally Due but Unpaid* noted as the reason for adjustment. This will ensure that an employee receives proper wage credit for the quarter when the wages should have been paid. However, the employment taxes due on these wages should be paid when the wages are actually or constructively paid for the employee.

Important:

- Wages are reported when they are paid to the employee, not when the employee earns the wages. Because UI and SDI benefits are based on the highest quarter of wages, it is important that wages are reported for the correct quarter. If you have any questions on reporting your employees' wages, contact the Taxpayer Assistance Center at 1-888-745-3886.

- **All employers are required to electronically submit employment tax returns, wage reports, and payroll tax deposits to the EDD.** Refer to page 49 for additional information on the e-file and e-pay mandate and related noncompliance penalties.

- A wage item penalty of **$20 per employee** will be charged for late reporting or unreported employee wages.

- A wage noncompliance penalty of **$20 per employee** will be charged for filing a paper wage report.

- Before submitting your DE 9C, make sure the following are correct:

  - The quarter you are reporting.
  - Your employer payroll tax account number.
  - The names of your employees, and their Social Security numbers.

Correcting a Previously Filed DE 9C

The DE 9C can be corrected through <u>e-Services for Business</u> (edd.ca.gov/eServices) even if originally filed using another electronic filing method or a paper form.

Online

Log in to <u>e-Services for Business</u> (edd.ca.gov/eServices) and access the previously filed DE 9C you want to correct. For step-by-step instructions:

- Refer to <u>How to Correct Prior Reports, Returns, or Deposits</u> (edd.ca.gov/en/payroll_taxes/how_to_correct_prior_ reports_or_deposits).

- Access the <u>*e-Services for Business User Guide* (DE160) (PDF)</u> (edd.ca.gov/pdf_pub_ctr/de160.pdf).

- View the <u>e-Services for Business Tutorials</u> (edd.ca.gov/en/payroll_taxes/e-Services_for_Business_Tutorials).

Paper

Complete and mail a DE 9ADJ. Refer to pages <u>65</u> and <u>66</u> for additional information and a DE 9ADJ sample form.

Required Forms

Go Paperless!
You can view or download this guide at <u>California Employer Guides</u>
(edd.ca.gov/en/Payroll_Taxes/Employers_Guides).

For the latest tax news and employer resources, visit
<u>California Employer News and Updates</u>
(edd.ca.gov/payroll_taxes/employer-news.htm).

Subscribe to the EDD no-cost <u>email subscription services</u>
(edd.ca.gov/about_edd/get_email_notices.htm).

Quarterly Contribution and Wage Adjustment Form (DE 9ADJ)

Overview

Employers use the *Quarterly Contribution and Wage Adjustment Form* (DE 9ADJ) to make corrections to previous tax returns and wage reports. Corrections can also be made electronically through e-Services for Business (edd.ca.gov/ eServices).

Refer to How to Correct Prior Reports, Returns, or Deposits (edd.ca.gov/en/payroll_taxes/how_to_correct_prior_ reports_or_deposits) for detailed instructions on how to request adjustments to the DE 9 and DE 9C through e-Services for Business or on paper adjustment forms.

The table below includes instructions on how to request adjustments on the paper DE 9ADJ. Detailed instructions are provided on the DE 9ADJ-I (PDF) (edd.ca.gov/pdf_pub_ctr/de9adji.pdf).

Type of Adjustment	How to Make an Adjustment
Reported incorrect UI, ETT, SDI, or PIT information on a **previously filed DE 9**.	• Complete sections I, II, III, and V of the DE 9ADJ. Also, complete section IV (items A and C) of the DE 9ADJ if a correction is needed to the DE 9C for the quarter. If an amount was overpaid, claim the amount overpaid in the **Total Taxes Due or Overpaid** field of your DE 9ADJ. If taxes are due, send a payment with the DE 9ADJ for the additional tax amount plus penalty and interest. To find current rates or to calculate interests visit Interest Rate on Overdue Taxes (edd.ca.gov/en/Payroll_Taxes/Interest_Rate). The penalty amount is 15% of the portion of the payment that is late.
Did not report employees on a **previously filed DE 9 and DE 9C**.	• Complete sections I, II, III, IV (items A and C), and V of the DE 9ADJ. • If taxes are due, send a payment with the **DE 9ADJ** for the additional tax amount plus penalty and interest. To find current rates or to calculate interests visit Interest Rate on Overdue Taxes (edd.ca.gov/en/Payroll_Taxes/Interest_Rate). The penalty amount is 15% of the portion of the payment that is late.
Reported employees on a **previously filed DE 9 and DE 9C** in error.	• Complete sections I, II, III, IV (items A and C), and V of the DE 9ADJ. If an amount was overpaid, claim the amount overpaid in the Total Taxes Due or Overpaid field of your DE 9ADJ.
Reported incorrect wages or PIT information on a **previously filed DE 9C**.	• Complete sections I, II, IV (items A and C), and V of the **DE 9ADJ**. Refer to pages 3 through 5 of the DE 9ADJ-I for detailed instructions and examples of wage line adjustments. Also, complete section III of the DE 9ADJ if a correction is needed to the DE 9 for the quarter. • If taxes are due, send a payment with the DE 9ADJ for the additional tax amount plus penalty and interest. To find current rates or to calculate interests visit Interest Rate on Overdue Taxes (edd.ca.gov/en/Payroll_Taxes/Interest_Rate). The penalty amount is 15% of the portion of the payment that is late.
Reported incorrect employee Social Security number (SSN) or name on a **previously filed DE 9C**.	Complete Sections I, II, IV (items A and C), and V of the DE 9ADJ. Refer to pages 3 through 5 of the DE 9ADJ-I for detailed instructions and examples of wage line adjustments.
No SSN reported for employees on a **previously filed DE 9C**.	Complete sections I, II, IV (items A and C), and V of the **DE 9ADJ**. Refer to pages 3 through 5 of the DE 9ADJ-I for detailed instructions and examples of wage line adjustments.
Incorrect wage plan codes reported on the **DE 9C**.	Complete sections I, II, IV (items A and B, or items A and C), and V. If correcting wage plan codes for all employees, complete items A and B in section IV. If correcting the wage plan codes for individual employees, complete Items A and C in section IV (C1 through C6 and C9) for each affected employee. Refer to the Information Sheet: *Reporting Wage Plan Codes on Quarterly Wage Reports and Adjusvtments* (DE 231WPC) (PDF) for information on wage plan codes and which wage plan code corrections do not need to be reported.

Contact the Taxpayer Assistance Center at 1-888-745-3886 for additional assistance.

A completed sample DE 9ADJ is shown on pages 66 and 67.

Required Forms

For Illustrative Purposes Only

Examples were created using 2023 rates.
Refer to inside front cover for 2024 rates.

Employment Development Department
State of California

Quarterly Contribution and Wage Adjustment Form

The *Quarterly Contribution and Wage Adjustment Form* (DE 9ADJ) is used to request corrections to information previously reported on a *Quarterly Contribution Return and Report of Wages* (DE 9) and/or *Quarterly Contribution Return and Report of Wages (Continuation)* (DE 9C). **A claim for refund** must be filed within 3 years of the last timely date of the quarter being adjusted, 6 months after an assessment becomes final, or 60 days from the date of the overpayment, whichever date occurs later.

You can also file adjustments to previously filed returns online through the Employment Development Department (EDD) e-Services for Business (edd.ca.gov/e-Services_for_Business). Refer to the *Instructions for Completing the Quarterly Contribution and Wage Adjustment Form (DE 9ADJ-I) (PDF)* (edd.ca.gov/pdf_pub_ctr/de9adji.pdf) for additional information.

Check the box that applies: ☐ If only adjusting the DE 9, complete Sections I, II, III, and V.   ☐ If only adjusting the DE 9C, complete Sections I, II, IV, and V.   ☑ If adjusting DE 9 and DE 9C, complete all sections.

Complete all fields (Please print).

SMITH

2345

Quarter 23/1

Employer Account Number
000-0000-0

Enter a detailed reason for the adjustments requested. (Required)

Required Forms

Section III: Request to Adjust the DE 9. Complete all fields. If requesting a credit (decrease) to SDI or PIT, you must also complete **Line O** below.	(1) Amounts Reported on DE 9 or Most Recent Adjustment Form	(2) Amounts That Should Have Been Reported	(3) Difference Debit/(Credit)
A. Total Subject Wages	9,000.00	18,500.50	9,500.50
B. Unemployment Insurance (UI) Taxable Wages	7,000.00	14,000.00	7,000.00
C. State Disability Insurance (SDI) Taxable Wages	9,000.00	18,500.50	9,500.50
D. Employer's UI Contributions (UI rate 3.4 % times B)	238.00	476.00	238.00
E. Employment Training Tax (ETT rate 0.1 % times B)	7.00	14.00	7.00
F. SDI Withheld (SDI rate 1.1 % times C) (Includes Paid Family Leave)	99.00	203.51	104.51
G. Personal Income Tax (PIT) Withheld	150.00	350.55	200.55
H. **Subtotal** (Add amounts on Lines D, E, F, and G)	494.00	1,044.06	550.06
I. Plus: Erroneous SDI Deductions Not Refunded (Refer to **Note** below)		0.00	
J. Less: Contributions and Withholdings Paid for the Quarter		494.00	
K. **Total Taxes Due or Overpaid** (H2 + I – J). (If balance is due, complete L, M, and N)		550.06	
L. Penalty (If balance is due, calculate 15% of the amount on Line K)		82.51	
M. Interest (Refer to the DE 9ADJ-I for instructions)		14.50	
N. **Total Due** (Lines K + L + M)		647.07	

O. **SDI and PIT overpayments.** If requesting a credit (decrease) to SDI or PIT, you must answer the following questions:

	SDI Deductions	PIT Deductions
1. Was the credit claimed above (column 3) withheld from the wages of employee(s)?	☐ Yes ☐ No	☐ Yes ☐ No
2. If yes, has this amount been refunded to the employee(s)?	☐ Yes ☐ No	☐ Yes ☐ No
3. Was the correct PIT reported on the Form W-2 issued to the employee(s)?		☐ Yes ☐ No

Note: SDI and PIT deductions are employee contributions. The EDD cannot refund these amounts unless you first refund the erroneous deductions to the employee(s). **If you have issued Form(s) W-2, do not refund PIT overwithholdings or change the amount reported on the employee(s) Form W-2.** The employee will receive a credit for the PIT overwithheld when they file their *California Income Tax Return* (Form 540) with the Franchise Tax Board. If you are requesting a PIT credit for a prior year because you paid the EDD more than the amount withheld from the employee(s), attach a copy of Form(s) W-2 filed for each affected employee. Refer to the DE 9ADJ-I for additional instructions.

Sign on Page 2 and Mail To: Employment Development Department / PO Box 989073 / West Sacramento, CA 95798-9073

DE 9ADJ Rev. 4 (1-23) **(INTERNET)**   Page 1 of _____   CU

Examples were created using 2023 rates. Refer to inside front cover for 2024 rates.

EDD Employment Development Department
State of California

Business Name: JOHN AND JANE SMITH

Quarter	Employer Account Number
23/1	000-0000-0

Section IV: Request to Adjust the DE 9C. Complete **Item A** for all DE 9C adjustments. Complete **Item B** only for wage plan code corrections to all employees. Complete **Item C** to request adjustments to individual employee information.

A. **DE 9C Grand Totals for the Quarter**

A1. Enter the correct grand totals for all employees for the quarter.

Total Subject Wages	Total PIT Wages	Total PIT Withheld
18,500.50	18,500.50	350.55

A2. Enter the number of employees full-time and part-time who worked during or received pay subject to UI for the pay period which includes the 12th of the month.

1st Month	2nd Month	3rd Month
1	2	2

A3. Enter the correct total number of wage lines **for all employees** for the quarter.

Wage Item Count
2

B. **Wage Plan Code Corrections for All Employees.** Leave blank if not correcting all wage plan codes. Refer to the *Information Sheet: Reporting Wage Plan Codes on Quarterly Wage Reports and Adjustments (DE 231WPC)* (PDF) (edd.ca.gov/pdf_pub_ctr/de231w. df) for additional information.

Enter Numbe.   Code: ____   Correct Plan Code: _____
(Item C   codes for all employees.)

C. **Individu   nent** type for each affected employee and complete the fields indica   rected. Make corrections to the quarter(s) in which the informatio   ative amounts.

File this form online through e-Services for Business (edd.ca.gov/eServices).

Adjustment	Fields to Complete for Each Affected Employee
Add employee(s).	C1 – C6. Leave C7 – C9 blank.
Remove employee(s) reported in error.	C1 – C6. Enter 0.00 in C3 – C5.
Adjust wages or PIT amounts previously reported.	C1 – C6. Leave C7 – C9 blank.
Correct employee name(s).	C1 – C6 and C7. Leave C8 – C9 blank.
Correct a Social Security number (SSN).	C1 – C6 and C8. Leave C7 and C9 blank.
Correct wage plan code for one or more employees but not all.	C1 – C6 and C9. Leave C7 and C8 blank.
Multiple adjustments.	C1 – C6 and C7 – C9 if they apply to adjustment.

Enter the information that **should have been reported** in fields C1 – C6. If a correction reduces wages or withholdings amount to zero, enter 0.00 in the field.				For name, SSN, or plan code corrections, enter the information **previously reported** in fields C7 – C9. Leave these fields blank for all other adjustment types.	
C1. Social Security Number (SSN) 000-00-0000	C2. Employee Name (First, Middle Initial, Last) THOMAS T TAYLOR			C7. Previously Reported Name (First, Middle Initial, Last)	
C3. Total Subject Wages 9,500.50	C4. PIT Wages 9,500.50	C5. PIT Withheld 200.55	C6. Plan Code S	C8. Previously Reported SSN	C9. Previously Reported Plan Code
C1. Social Security Number (SSN) 000-00-0000	C2. Employee Name (First, Middle Initial, Last) HARRY L JONES			C7. Previously Reported Name (First, Middle Initial, Last) HAROLD L JONES	
C3. Total Subject Wages 9,000.00	C4. PIT Wages 9,000.00	C5. PIT Withheld 150.00	C6. Plan Code S	C8. Previously Reported SSN 000-00-0000	C9. Previously Reported Plan Code
C1. Social Security Number (SSN)	C2. Employee Name (First, Middle Initial, Last)			C7. Previously Reported Name (First, Middle Initial, Last)	
C3. Total Subject Wages	C4. PIT Wages	C5. PIT Withheld	C6. Plan Code	C8. Previously Reported SSN	C9. Previously Reported Plan Code

Please attach additional pages if reporting more than 3 wage line adjustments.

Section V: Declaration. I declare that the information herein is true and correct to the best of my knowledge. (A signature is required on all adjustments)

Signature *Jane Smith*   Title OWNER   Date 01/02/2024

Print Name Jane Smith   Phone (123) 555-7899   Email Jane123@gmail.com

Sign and Mail To: Employment Development Department / PO Box 989073 / West Sacramento, CA 95798-9073

DE 9ADJ Rev. 4 (1-23) **(INTERNET)**   Page 2 of _____

Required Forms

Federal Forms W-2 and 1099

Wage and Tax Statement (Form W-2)

Employers are required to annually prepare a federal *Wage and Tax Statement* (Form W-2) for each employee. For tax year 2024, employers must provide each employee with a Form W-2 by January 31, 2025.* Prepare the Form W-2 on the federal and state four-part paper form. To obtain these forms, visit the IRS (irs.gov).

For information on Form W-2 reporting requirements, refer to the IRS *Employer's Tax Guide* (Publication 15, Circular E) (irs.gov/publications/p15). For federal instructions on completing Form W-2, refer to the IRS publication *2024 General Instructions for Forms W-2 and W-3*. To obtain these publications, visit the IRS (irs.gov) or call the IRS at 1-800-829-3676.

In addition to required federal information, employers must include PIT wages, PIT withheld, and SDI tax withheld in the following Form W-2 boxes:

Form W-2	
Box	**Enter**
Box 16 (state wages, tips, etc.)	California PIT wages
Box 17 (state income tax)	California PIT withheld
Box 19 (local income tax)	The abbreviation *CASDI* or SDI withheld (For additional information, refer to *Note* below.)

Note: If Box 19 has local taxes, use *Box 14-Other*. If no boxes are available, you are required to provide your employees with a separate written statement containing:

- Your business or entity name, address, federal employer identification number, and the Employment Development Department (EDD) eight-digit employer payroll tax account number.
- The employee's name, address, state, and Social Security number.
- The amount of SDI tax withheld or paid directly by you under the state plan.
- If the wages were not subject to SDI, show *CASDI 0* (zero).
- If you pay SDI taxes without withholding SDI from the employee's wages, you should show the SDI taxes as if withheld and increase the amount you report according to the formula as shown on *Information Sheet: Social Security, Medicare, State Disability Insurance, Federal Income Taxes Paid by an Employer* (DE 231Q). Download the DE 231Q (PDF) (edd.ca.gov/pdf_pub_ctr/de231q.pdf) or contact the Taxpayer Assistance Center at 1-888-745-3886.
- If you are covered under an authorized Voluntary Plan Disability Insurance (VPDI), enter VPDI and the VPDI amount withheld.

Generally, the amount reported as California PIT wages on Form W-2 (Box 16, State wages) is the same as the federal wages (Box 1). However, the amounts may differ based on:

- Federal and California differences in definition of:
  - Employee (refer to *Information Sheet: Types of Employment* [DE 231TE]).
  - Taxable wages (refer to *Information Sheet: Types of Payments* [DE 231TP]).
  - The DE 231TE and DE 231TP are available on Forms and Publications (edd.ca.gov/payroll_taxes/ forms_and_publications.htm) or contact the Taxpayer Assistance Center at 1-888-745-3886.
- Residency of the employee (refer to page 16).
- If the employee performs services in more than one state.

For additional information on federal and California differences, contact the Taxpayer Assistance Center at 1-888-745-3886. If the employee performs services in more than one state, contact the other state(s) for guidance on how to complete the Form W-2 for that state.

If you discover an error on a previously issued Form W-2, refer to the IRS publication *General Instructions for Forms W-2C and W-3C* for guidance on completing an IRS *Corrected Wage and Tax Statement* (Form W-2C). To obtain these forms, visit the IRS (irs.gov) or call 1-800-829-3676.

*Employers failing to provide a Form W-2 to each employee, or who provide a false or fraudulent statement, are subject to a **penalty of fifty dollars ($50)** for each such failure as imposed pursuant to section 13052 of the California Unemployment Insurance Code (CUIC). Employers may also be subject to an additional penalty for failure to file informational returns (Form W-2, Form 1099-MISC, or Form 1099-NEC) to misclassified employees as provided pursuant to section 13052.5 of the CUIC. The amount of the penalty is determined based upon the unreported payments for personal services multiplied by the maximum rate as provided pursuant to section 17041 of the Revenue and Taxation Code. Contact the EDD Taxpayer Assistance Center at 1-888-745-3886 for assistance.

Federal Forms W-2 and 1099 continued

Do not send a copy of Form W-2 or Form W-2C to the State of California Employment Development Department (EDD) or the Franchise Tax Board (FTB). Forms W-2 and W-2C are not filed with the state because you should already be reporting wage and withholding information to the EDD on the *Quarterly Contribution Return and Report of Wages (Continuation)* (DE 9C). However, you must continue to send Forms W-2 and W-2C to your employees and the Social Security Administration.

Information Return (Forms 1099-MISC and 1099-NEC)

Individuals, partnerships, corporations, or other organizations engaged in a trade or business in California may have a requirement to report independent contractor payments made in the course of their business. For 2024, you must provide a statement to each independent contractor by January 31, 2025*, containing the information provided to the IRS and FTB. If you do not use the official IRS Form 1099-MISC or 1099-NEC to provide the statement to recipients, refer to the IRS Publication 1179 (irs.gov/forms-pubs/about-publication-1179) for specific rules for substitute statements.

How to File

FTB recommends that you file under the IRS Combined Federal and State Filing program. When you are approved and use the IRS Combined Federal/State Filing program, you only have to file once. The IRS will forward your California information returns to FTB. The following forms may be filed under this program: Forms 1099-DIV, 1099-G, 1099-INT, 1099-MISC, 1099-NEC, 1099-OID, 1099-PATR, 1099-R, and 5498. For information on the IRS Combined Federal and State Filing program, call the IRS at 1-866-455-7438.

If you are not participating in the Combined Federal and State Filing program, did not file by paper with the IRS, and file 250 or more information returns of one type, you must file electronically directly with FTB. If you file less than 250 returns, you must file either by paper or electronically with FTB.

If you file paper information returns with the IRS, **do not send a paper copy to FTB**: The IRS will forward the information to FTB. This applies to paper filing only.

Generally, FTB's reporting requirements are the same as the IRS reporting requirements. For specific differences, contact the Information Reporting Program Help Desk at irphelp@ftb.ca.gov.

Publications and Contact Information

Visit the IRS (irs.gov) to obtain Form 1099 reporting requirements and instructions, the IRS Publication 1220, and the IRS General Instructions for Forms 1099, 1098, 5498, and W-2G, or call 1-800-829-3676.

Note: California PIT withheld from pension, annuity, and other deferred income should be reported on the IRS form *Distributions From Pensions, Annuities, Retirement or Profit-Sharing Plans, IRAs, Insurance Contracts, etc.* (Form 1099-R). For instructions on completing Form 1099-R, refer to IRS Instructions for Forms 1099-R and 5498. To obtain instructions, visit the IRS (irs.gov) or call the IRS at 1-800-829-3676.

For more information, contact:

Internal Revenue Services
1-866-455-7438
irs.gov
mccirp@irs.gov

Franchise Tax Board
ftb.ca.gov
irphelp@ftb.ca.gov

*Failure to provide an *Information Return* (Form 1099), if required, may result in a penalty for each independent contractor as imposed pursuant to section 13052.5 of the California Unemployment Insurance Code or section 19175 of the Revenue and Taxation Code (R&TC). The amount of the penalty is the unreported payments for personal services multiplied by the maximum rate as provided pursuant to section 17041 of the R&TC. Contact the EDD Taxpayer Assistance Center at 1-888-745-3886 for assistance.

Note: All employers are required to notify all of their employees of the federal Earned Income Tax Credit. Refer to page 73 for details.

Change to Your Business Status

Registered employers must report any change in business status to the EDD. Employers or their authorized representative may report changes to an employer payroll tax account using e-Services for Business (edd.ca.gov/eServices).

Business Name and Mailing Address Change

If you have changes to your business such as:

- Your business name.
- Corporation name.
- Personal name (for example, marriage).
- Change in ownership of the business.
- Business mailing address.

➡️ **Action Required:**

Notify the EDD of any change to your business status through e-Services for Business (edd.ca.gov/eServices).

No Longer Have Employees

If you no longer have employees and will not be reporting wages in any future quarter, you must **submit a final DE 88, DE 9, and DE 9C**. You may close your employer payroll tax account using e-Services for Business (edd.ca.gov/eServices). For instructions on how to reopen your Employer Payroll Tax Account, visit the e-Services for Business FAQs (edd.ca.gov/en/payroll_taxes/faq_-_e-services_for_business) category Register, Close, or Reopen an Employer Payroll Tax Account.

If you currently do not have employees, but may have employees in future quarters, you are **required to file your DE 9 and DE 9C stating you have no payroll to report every quarter**, otherwise the EDD may presume you have employees and assess your account.

Close Your Business

If you close your business, you are **required to submit a final DE 88, DE 9, and DE 9C within 10 days** of quitting business, **regardless** of the normal due dates. You must close your employer payroll tax account using e-Services for Business (edd.ca.gov/eServices). For instructions on how to reopen your Employer Payroll Tax Account, visit the e-Services for Business FAQs (edd.ca.gov/en/payroll_taxes/faq_-_e-services_for_business) category Register, Close, or Reopen an Employer Payroll Tax Account.

Reopen Your Employer Payroll Tax Account

Request to reopen your employer tax account on e-Services for Business (edd.ca.gov/eServices) if:

- You paid wages in excess of $100 in the current calendar year or within the preceding calendar year and pay wages in any amount in the current calendar year.

- You **did not** have payroll in the preceding calendar year and you paid wages in excess of $100 in any calendar quarter in the current calendar year.

Purchase, Sell, Transfer, or Change Ownership

Registered employers must report any change in business status. For example, any change in business name or legal entity, such as a change from partnership or limited liability company to corporation. Report changes through e-Services for Business (edd.ca.gov/eServices).

If you add or remove partners or LLC members; change corporate name or officers of a business entity type, the entity normally keeps the same EDD employer payroll tax account number and continues to make payroll tax deposits and file reports as though it was the same type of ownership for the entire year. The EDD must be notified of any change in the ownership of a business entity so that the taxpayer information can be updated. For additional information, contact the Taxpayer Assistance Center at 1-888-745-3886. If outside the U.S. or Canada, call 1-916-464-3502.

Remember: Report changes through e-Services for business (edd.ca.gov/eServices).

Purchase a Business

If you purchase a business with employees, or a business that previously had employees, you may be held liable for the previous owner's EDD liability if a *Certificate of Release of Buyer* (DE 2220) is not obtained. To request a DE 2220, contact the Taxpayer Assistance Center at 1-888-745-3886. If outside the U.S. or Canada, call 1-916-464-3502.

Until a DE 2220 is issued, you, the buyer, must hold in escrow an amount sufficient to cover all amounts the seller owes to the EDD, up to the purchase price of the business. The DE 2220 is issued after the seller pays all amounts owed to the EDD. Payment must be made by cash, cashier's check, certified check, escrow check, or money order payable to the Employment Development Department.

For your protection, escrow funds should not be disbursed until the DE 2220 has been issued. For additional information, download the *Requirements for Obtaining Certificate of Release of Buyer (DE 2220) When a Business Is Sold* (DE 3409A) (PDF) (edd.ca.gov/pdf_pub_ctr/de3409a.pdf) or contact the Taxpayer Assistance Center at 1-888-745-3886. If outside the U.S. or Canada, call 1-916-464-3502.

Note: If you employ any of the former owner's workers immediately after the acquisition of the business, the wages paid to these employees during the same calendar year are considered as having been paid by you. Therefore, wages paid by the former owner in the current calendar year are applied to the taxable wage limits for Unemployment Insurance tax, Employment Training Tax, and State Disability Insurance tax.

What Is A Successor Employer?

A successor employer is an employer who has acquired all or part of another employer's predecessor's business and continues to operate the business without substantial reduction of personnel resulting from the acquisition. The successor employer may receive all or part of the predecessor's UI reserve account balance by applying for a reserve account transfer. The transfer may result in an immediate reduction or increase of the successor's UI tax rate. The successor employer must register the acquired business with the EDD.

For more information on reserve account transfers, refer to page 81 or call 1-916-653-7795.

Note: Acquiring all or part of the stock in a corporation does not constitute a new employing unit. The corporation retains the same EDD employer payroll tax account number.

It Is Against the Law to Change or Purchase a Business Entity Solely to Obtain a Lower UI Rate

Changing your business ownership solely for the purpose of obtaining an employer account with a lower UI contribution rate is not allowed. Section 1052 of the California Unemployment Insurance Code provides that a reserve account transfer will not apply to any acquisition, which is determined to have been made for the purpose of obtaining a more favorable UI contribution rate. The EDD aggressively pursues businesses practicing UI rate manipulation. To read more about UI rate manipulation, refer to page 83.

Change of Status

Additional Requirements

Posting Requirements

Once you are registered with the EDD, you will receive a notice to post in your workplace that informs your employees of their rights under Unemployment Insurance (UI), Disability Insurance (DI), and Paid Family Leave (PFL). This notice must be posted in a prominent location that is easily seen by your employees. You will receive the following notice if you are subject to:

- UI, DI, and PFL – *Notice to Employees* (DE 1857A).

- UI only – *Notice to Employees - Unemployment Insurance Benefits* (DE 1857D).

- DI and PFL only – *Notice to Employees* (DE 1858).

Required Notices and Pamphlets

Provide a copy of the following notices and pamphlets to each of your employees when appropriate. The publications listed below are available at <u>Required Notices and Pamphlets</u> (edd.ca.gov/payroll_taxes/required_ notices_and_pamphlets.htm).

- The following pamphlets explain your employees' benefit rights:
- *For Your Benefit*: *California's Programs for the Unemployed* (DE 2320) – Provides information on UI, DI, PFL, and Workforce Services benefits available to the employee and must be given when an employer discharges, lays off, or places an employee on a leave of absence. Printed copies of this notice may be provided to employees in person or via mail. Notice may also be provided via email if the following requirements are met:
  - Employers may provide this notice via email if an employee affirmatively opts into receipt of electronic statements or materials.
  - An employee may consent to receive electronic communication in writing, by email, or by some form of electronic acknowledgement.
  - In the case of electronic acknowledgement, the acknowledgement form must:
    - Fully explain that the employee agrees to receive notice electronically;
    - Provide the employee with information about how they can revoke consent of electronic receipt; and
    - Create a record of the agreement which can be provided to the employee.
  - Employees may revoke the agreement to receive notice by electronic communication at any time in writing, by email, or by some form of electronic acknowledgement.
- *Disability Insurance Provisions* (DE 2515) – Provides information on DI benefits.

- *Paid Family Leave Brochure* (DE 2511) – Provides information on PFL benefits.

Note: For additional information on your posting requirements, visit the <u>California Tax Service Center</u> (taxes.ca.gov). Voluntary Plan Disability Insurance (VPDI) insurers have similar literature. VPDI employers must also supply claim forms to their employees. For more information on VPDI, refer to <u>page 95</u>.

- Notice required by the Earned Income Tax Credit Information Act (refer to <u>page 73</u> for details).

- Notice to Employee as to Change in Relationship – Written notice must be given immediately to employees of their discharge, layoff, leave of absence, or change in employment status, along with a DE 2320.

- Notice of plant closure or mass layoff.

> 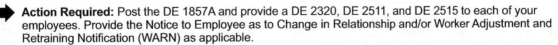 **Action Required:** Post the DE 1857A and provide a DE 2320, DE 2511, and DE 2515 to each of your employees. Provide the Notice to Employee as to Change in Relationship and/or Worker Adjustment and Retraining Notification (WARN) as applicable.

No written notice is required if it is a voluntary quit, promotion or demotion, change in work assignment or location (some changes in location require a WARN notice), or if work stopped due to a trade dispute.

Additional Requirements continued

Notices prepared by you **must** include the information as shown.
The following sample meets the requirements:

NOTICE TO EMPLOYEE AS TO CHANGE IN RELATIONSHIP

(Issued pursuant to provisions of section 1089 of the California Unemployment Insurance Code.)

Name _____   SSN _____

1. You were/will be laid off/discharged on _____ , 20 _____
                                                          (date)

2. You were/will be on leave of absence starting _____ , 20 _____
                                                                    (date)

3. On _____ , your employment status changed/will change as follows:
              (date)

_____
(Name of Employer)

_____
(By)

Earned Income Tax Credit Information Act

The refundable California Earned Income Tax Credit (California EITC) is available to low-income working individuals who earned wage income subject to California withholding or have net earnings from self-employment. This credit is similar to the federal Earned Income Credit (EIC) but with different income limitations. To claim the California EITC, you must file a California income tax return and attach a completed *California Earned Income Tax Credit* (FTB 3514) form. For information on the availability of the credit, eligibility requirements, and how to obtain the necessary California tax forms or get help filing, visit the <u>Franchise Tax Board</u> (ftb.ca.gov/forms) or call 1-800-852-5711.

Employers who are subject to, and required to provide, unemployment insurance to their employees must provide EITC notification to the employee by either handing it directly to the employee, mailing it to the employee's last known address, or providing it via email if an employee opts into receipt of electronic statements or materials. Posting of this information on an employee bulletin board will not satisfy the notification requirement.

The notification will be provided within one week before, after, or during the time the employer provides an annual wage summary, including, but not limited to, Forms W-2 or 1099, to the employee. The notice will include instructions on how to obtain any notices available from the IRS and FTB for this purpose, including, but not limited to, the IRS Notice 797 and information on the California EITC or any successor notice or form, or any notice created by you as long as it contains substantially the same language as the notice below.

> "Based on your annual earnings, you may be eligible to receive the Earned Income Tax Credit (EITC) from the federal government. The EITC is a refundable federal income tax credit for low-income working individuals and families. EITC has no effect on certain welfare benefits. In most cases, earned income tax credit payments will not be used to determine eligibility for Medicaid, supplemental security income, food stamps, low-income housing, or most temporary assistance for needy families' payments. Even if you do not owe federal taxes, you must file a tax return to receive the earned income tax credit. Be sure to fill out the EITC form in the federal income tax return booklet. For information regarding your eligibility to receive the EITC, including information on how to obtain the IRS Notice 797, or any other necessary forms and instructions, visit the <u>IRS</u> (irs.gov) or contact the IRS at 1-800-829-3676."

You also may be eligible to receive the California EITC starting with the calendar year 2015 tax year. The California EITC is a refundable state income tax credit for low-income working individuals and families. The California EITC is treated in the same manner as the federal EITC and generally will not be used to determine eligibility for welfare benefits under California law. To claim the California EITC, even if you do not owe California taxes, you must file a California income tax return and complete and attach the California EITC form (FTB 3514). For information on the availability of the credit, eligibility requirements, and how to obtain the necessary California forms and get help filing, contact the Franchise Tax Board at 1-800-852-5711 or visit the Franchise Tax Board website at <u>ftb.ca.gov</u>.

Plant Closure or Mass Layoff

Federal and California Worker Adjustment and Retraining Notification (WARN) laws require covered employers to provide 60 days advance notice of plant closings and mass layoffs. Advance notice provides employees and their families some transition time to adjust to the prospective loss of employment, to seek and obtain alternative jobs, and, if necessary, to acquire skill training or retraining that will allow these employees to successfully compete in the job market.

Employers should review the Federal WARN law and the California WARN law Labor Code section 1400—1408 for a full understanding of the notification requirements. The California WARN law also applies to an employer who is relocating a call center as defined in California Labor Code section 1409-1413.

For more information on WARN requirements visit WARN Information for employers (edd.ca.gov/Jobs_and_Training/ Layoff_Services_WARN.htm) or the federal WARN Act Compliance Assistance (edd.ca.gov/en/Jobs_and_Training/ Layoff_Services_WARN).

General Provisions of the Federal and California WARN Laws

Category	Federal WARN	California WARN
Covered Employers	Applicable only to employers with 100 or more full-time employees who must have been employed for at least six months of the 12 months preceding the date of required notice in order to be counted. (29 United States Code [USC] 2101 and 20 Code Federal Regulations [CFR] 639.3)	Applicable to a *covered establishment* that employs or has employed in the preceding 12 months 75 or more full and part-time employees. As under the federal WARN Act, employees must have been employed for at least six months of the 12 months preceding the date of required notice in order to be counted. (California Labor Code, section 1400.5[a] and [h])
Plant Closing or Layoff Requiring Notice	Plant closings involving 50 or more employees during a 30-day period. Layoffs within a 30-day period involving 50 to 499 full-time employees constituting at least 33 percent of the full-time workforce at a single site of employment. Layoffs of 500 or more employees are covered regardless of percentage of workforce. (29 USC, et seq., 2101 and 20 CFR 639.3)	Plant closure affecting any amount of employees. Layoff of 50 or more employees within a 30-day period regardless of percent of workforce. Relocation of at least 100 miles affecting any amount of employees. (California Labor Code section 1400.5 [d]-[f])
Legal Jurisdiction	Enforcement of WARN requirements through U.S. District Courts. The court, in its discretion, may allow the prevailing party a reasonable attorney's fee as part of the costs. (29 USC 2101, et seq.)	Suit may be brought in *any court of competent jurisdiction*. The court may award reasonable attorney's fees as part of costs to any prevailing plaintiff. The California WARN law is in the Labor Code, and the authority to investigate through the examination of books and records is delegated to the Labor Commissioner. (California Labor Code, sections 1404 and 1406)
Employer Liability	An employer who violates the WARN provisions is liable to each employee for an amount equal to back pay and benefits for the period of the violation, up to 60 days, but no more than half the number of days the employee was employed by the employer. (29 USC; 2104[a])	A possible civil penalty of $500 a day for each day of violation. Employees may receive back pay to be paid at employee's final rate or three-year average rate of compensation, whichever is higher. In addition, employer is liable for cost of any medical expenses incurred by employees that would have been covered under an employee benefit plan. The employer is liable for a period of violation up to 60 days or one-half the number of days the employee was employed whichever period is smaller. (California Labor Code, section 1403)

Additional Requirements

Plant Closure or Mass Layoff – WARN

Category	Federal WARN	California WARN

Notice Requirements	An employer must provide written notice 60 days prior to a plant closing or mass layoff to all of the following:
	
	• Employees or their representative.
	• Employment Development Department.
	   ○ Email a WARN Notice to WARNNotice@edd.ca.gov.
	• The chief elected official of local government within which such closing or layoff is to occur.
	
	(29 USC, 2102; 20 CFR 639.5 and 639.6)
		An employer must give notice 60 days prior to a plant closing, layoff, or relocation. In addition to the notifications required under the federal WARN Act, notice must also be given to both of the following:
		
		• The Local Workforce Development Board.
		• Employment Development Department.
		   ○ Email a WARN Notice to WARNNotice@edd.ca.gov.
		• The chief elected official of each city and county government within which the termination, relocation, or mass layoff occurs.
		
		(California Labor Code, section 1401)

Exceptions and Exemptions to Notice Requirements	Regular federal, state, local, and federally recognized Indian tribal governments are not covered. (20 CFR 639.3) **The following situations are exempt from notice:** • There is an offer to transfer employee to a different site within a reasonable commuting distance. (29 USC, 2101[b][2]; 20 CFR 639.5) • The closure is due to unforeseeable business circumstances or a natural disaster. (29 USC, 2103; 20 CFR 639.9) • The closing or layoff constitutes a strike or constitutes a lockout not intended to evade the requirement of this chapter. (29 USC, 2103[2])	California WARN law does not apply when the closing or layoff is the result of the completion of a particular project or undertaking of an employer subject to Wage Orders 11, 12, or 16, regulating the Motion Picture Industry, or Construction, Drilling, Logging, and Mining Industries, and the employees were hired with the understanding that their employment was limited to the duration of that project or undertaking. (California Labor Code, section 1400.5[g]) The notice requirements do not apply to employees involved in seasonal employment where the employees were hired with the understanding that their employment was seasonal and temporary. (California Labor Code, section 1400.5[g][2]) Notice is not required if a mass layoff, relocation, or plant closure is necessitated by a physical calamity or act of war. (California Labor Code, section 1401[c]) Notice of a relocation or termination is not required where, under multiple and specific conditions, the employer submits documents to the Department of Industrial Relations (DIR), and DIR determines that the employer was actively seeking capital or business, and a WARN notice would have precluded the employer from obtaining the capital or business. (California Labor Code, section 1402.5). This exception does not apply to notice of a mass layoff as defined in California Labor Code section 1400.5(d). (California Labor Code, section 1402.5[d])

Rapid Response is a proactive, business-focused program to assist companies facing potential layoffs or plant closures. Rapid Response Teams provide early intervention assistance to help avert potential layoffs and assist workers facing job losses. They provide important information about the services available under the Workforce Innovation and Opportunity Act and the EDD Workforce Services and UI programs.

If the dislocation is the result of foreign trade, the dislocated worker may be eligible for Trade Adjustment Assistance (TAA) services such as assistance with job search, training and case management services. For more information about the TAA program, refer to page 97. To learn more about Rapid Response services, contact the Local Workforce Area (edd.ca.gov/en/jobs_and_training/Local_Area_Listing) near you.

Additional Requirements

U.S. Government Contractor Job Listing Requirements

Nationally, employers with U.S. government contracts or subcontracts who meet the criteria listed in the table below are required to list job openings with the state workforce agency job bank, which in California is known as CalJOBS℠ (caljobs.ca.gov). This is required to enable the EDD to comply with federal compliance inquiries from the Office of Federal Contractor Compliance Program (OFCCP). Contractors may post their job openings on the National Labor Exchange (NLx) (usnlx.com), however, CalJOBS℠ does not maintain permanent records of jobs imported from the NLx or other third-party job sites. Furthermore, employers are required to take affirmative action to employ and advance in employment, qualified disabled veterans, other protected veterans, Armed Forces service medal veterans, and recently separated veterans. They must also file an annual VETS-4212 Federal Contract Reporting with the U.S. Department of Labor to disclose the total number of current employees in each job category and at each hiring location. For more information, visit the U.S. Department of Labor (dol.gov/agencies/vets/programs/vets4212).

The table below provides the general provisions of the Federal Contractor Reporting requirements.

Subject	Subject Prior to December 1, 2003	On or After December 1, 2003
Job Listings	Employers with a federal government contract of $25,000 or more, prior to December 1, 2003, and not modified on or after December 1, 2003, if more than $100,000, must list applicable job openings with the state National Labor Exchange website. In California, employers must first register and list applicable jobs within CalJOBS℠. (41 CFR 60-250.40)	Government contractors with a federal government contract of $150,000 or more, must list applicable job openings with the state workforce agency job bank (CalJOBS℠ in California), or the local American Job Center (known as the employment service delivery system) where the openings occur. Listing these employment openings is one type of affirmative action the contractor takes to recruit and hire qualified veterans. The contractor has some immediate actions to take as soon as it has a minimum threshold contract, and it has some ongoing actions it must take for as long as it continues to be a federal contractor subject to the Vietnam Era Veteran's Readjustment Assistance Act. For more information, refer to the Postings and Notice Requirements (dol. gov/sites/dolgov/files/ofccp/CAGuides/files/Postings&NoticesGuide-CONTR508c.pdf).
VETS-4212 Federal Contract Reporting	Employers with a federal government contract of $25,000 or more, entered into prior to December 1, 2003, and not modified on or after December 1, 2003, if more than $100,000, must file a VETS-4212 Federal Contract Reporting. (38 United States Code, sections 4211 and 4212)	Employers with a federal government contract of $150,000 or more entered into or modified on or after December 1, 2003, must file a VETS-4212 Federal Contract Reporting. (38 United States Code, sections 4211 and 4212)
Affirmative Action Program	Employers with a federal government contract of $50,000 or more, entered into prior to December 1, 2003, and not modified on or after December 1, 2003, if more than $100,000 and have 50 or more employees, must prepare, implement, and maintain a written Affirmative Action Plan for each of its establishments. (41 CFR 60-250.40)	Government contractors with a federal government contract of $150,000 or more, must prepare, implement, and maintain a written Affirmative Action Plan for each of its establishments. (41 CFR 60-300.40)

Additional Requirements

Recordkeeping

Employers are required to keep payroll records for at least four years. If you believe that you are not a subject employer or that your employees are exempt, state law requires that you maintain records of payments made to people who provide services to your business for at least eight years in case of an employment tax audit. Your records must provide a true and accurate account of all workers (employed, no longer employed, on a leave of absence, and independent contractors) and all payments made. Records must include the following information for each worker:

- Worker's:
  - Full name (first name, middle initial, and last name).
  - Social Security number.

- Date hired, rehired, or returned to work after a temporary layoff.

- Last date services were performed.

- Place of work.

- Monies paid:
  - Dates and amounts of payment.
  - Pay period covered.

- Cash or cash value of in-kind wages such as meals, lodging, bonuses, gifts, and prizes, showing the nature of the payment, the period that the services were performed, and the type of special payment made.

- The amounts withheld from employee wages. (**Note:** You may be required to make withholding deposits. Refer to Withholding Deposits on page 58.)

- Disbursement records showing payments to workers.

- Other information necessary to determine payments to workers.

If you have any questions on the records you must keep, refer to the *Information Sheet: Employment Tax Audit Process* (DE 231TA) (PDF) (edd.ca.gov/pdf_pub_ctr/de231ta.pdf) or by contacting the Taxpayer Assistance Center at 1-888-745-3886.

For the latest tax news and employer resources, visit
California Employer News and Updates
(edd.ca.gov/payroll_taxes/employer-news.htm).

Subscribe to the EDD no-cost email subscription services
(edd.ca.gov/about_edd/get_email_notices.htm).

Additional Requirements

Employers' Bill of Rights

Commitment

The Employment Development Department (EDD) is committed to applying the payroll tax laws of the State of California in an equitable and impartial manner. We developed the following to inform you of your rights during the employment taxation process.

Employer Rights

As an employer, you have the right to:

- Courteous and timely service from EDD employees.
- Expect that information maintained by the EDD be kept confidential and not published or made available for public inspection. However, in certain instances, the law requires that this information be shared with other governmental agencies. When those instances occur, the EDD closely follows the law to protect your rights to confidentiality.
- Call upon the EDD for accurate information, assistance, and to have all your questions answered.
- Receive a clear and accurate account statement if the EDD believes you owe taxes.
- Request a filing extension for up to 60 days. The law provides that the EDD may grant a filing extension where *good cause* is shown for a delay. (Refer to page 109 for the definition of *good cause*.)
- Request a filing extension for up to 60 days. The law provides that the EDD may grant a filing extension when the governor declares a state of emergency if the employer is directly affected by an emergency or disaster.
- Request a waiver of penalty by showing *good cause* for filing a report or making a late payment.
- An impartial audit and a full explanation of our findings if your business is selected for an audit.
- Discuss the issues with an EDD representative, supervisor, office manager, and the Taxpayer Advocate Office if you disagree with an action taken by the EDD.
- Appeal certain actions to the California Unemployment Insurance Appeals Board.

The *Employers' Bill of Rights (DE 195) (PDF)* (edd.ca.gov/pdf_pub_ctr/de195.pdf) brochure has been developed to inform you of your rights during the employment taxation process. For more information contact the Taxpayer Assistance Center at 1-888-745-3886.

Office of the Taxpayer Rights Advocate

The EDD Tax Branch established the Office of the Taxpayer Rights Advocate (OTRA), which is responsible for providing a clear and consistent focus on protecting the rights of the taxpayer. Incorporated within OTRA are the Taxpayer Advocate Office and the Settlements Office.

Taxpayer Advocate Office

The Taxpayer Advocate Office is responsible for protecting the rights of taxpayers during all phases of the payroll tax administration, assessment, and collection process, while also protecting the interests of the state.

If you are unable to resolve a payroll tax problem with an EDD representative, supervisor, and office manager, you may contact the Taxpayer Advocate Office for assistance. This office will review the issues and facts of your case to ensure that your rights have been protected and work to facilitate a resolution.

Employment Development Department
Tax Branch, MIC 93
Taxpayer Advocate Office
PO Box 826880
Sacramento, CA 94280-0001

Toll-free Phone: 1-866-594-4177
Phone: 1-916-654-8957
Fax: 1-916-449-9498

Office of the Taxpayer Rights Advocate continued

Settlements Office

The Settlements Program provides employers and the state an opportunity to avoid the cost of prolonged litigation associated with resolving disputed payroll tax issues (for example, petitions for reassessment, appeals, or denial of refund claims).

When reviewing a settlement offer, the EDD considers the risks and costs for the state associated with litigating the issues, balanced against the benefit of reaching a settlement agreement. Final tax liabilities, cases still in process, cases involving fraud or criminal violations, and issues solely involving fairness or financial hardship are generally not eligible. Depending on the reduction of tax and penalties, all settlement agreements are subject to approval by an Administrative Law Judge, the California Unemployment Insurance Appeals Board, and/or the Attorney General's office. If you have questions, refer to the *Information Sheet: Settlements Program* (DE 231SP) (PDF) (edd.ca.gov/siteassets/files/pdf_pub_ctr/de231sp.pdf) or contact the Settlement Office at 1-916-653-9130 or the Taxpayer Assistance Center at 1-888-745-3886.

Settlement offers must be in writing. You can email, fax, or mail in your settlement offers to the Settlements Office:

taxtsdsg@edd.ca.gov
Fax: 1-916-449-2161

Employment Development Department
Settlements Office, MIC 93
PO Box 826880
Sacramento, CA 94280-0001

Protecting Your Privacy

The EDD recognizes that your privacy is a personal and fundamental right without exception. We value and protect your privacy, and place strict controls on the gathering and use of personally identifiable data. Your personal information is not disclosed, made available, or otherwise used for purposes other than those specified at or before the time of collection, except with your consent or as authorized by law or regulation.

Payroll tax and benefit information collected and maintained by the EDD is confidential. As an employer, you have the right to obtain access to and inspect your records. You may also authorize your agent or representative to access your records by submitting a *Power of Attorney (POA) Declaration* (DE 48) (PDF) (edd.ca.gov/pdf_pub_ctr/de48.pdf) online through e-Services for Business (edd.ca.gov/eServices) or by contacting the Taxpayer Assistance Center at 1-888-745-3886.

If you have further questions regarding your privacy rights, contact the Tax Information Security Office at 1-916-654-5981.

Offers in Compromise

An Offer in Compromise (OIC) enables a qualified applicant to reduce an employment tax liability to less than full value. To qualify for an OIC, all of the following are required:

- The liability must be final and undisputed.

- The employer's account must be inactive and out-of-business or the applicant must no longer have a controlling interest or any association with the business that incurred the liability.

- The applicant must meet all financial requirements.

- Full financial disclosure is required before an offer can be analyzed.

If you have questions, refer to the *Information Sheet: Offers in Compromise* (DE 631C) (PDF) (edd.ca.gov/siteassets/files/pdf_pub_ctr/de631c.pdf) or contact the OIC office at 1-916-464-2739.

Unemployment Insurance – Taxes

The Unemployment Insurance (UI) program provides financial assistance to individuals who are temporarily out of work through no fault of their own. In California, this program is financed entirely by employers.

Methods of Paying for UI Benefits

Experience Rating Method

The experience rating method is used by most of employers. For a detailed explanation of the experience rating method, refer to the "How Your UI Tax Rate Is Determined" section below, obtain *Information Sheet: California System of Experience Rating (DE 231Z) (PDF)* (edd.ca.gov/pdf_pub_ctr/de231z.pdf), or contact the Taxpayer Assistance Center at 1-888-745-3886.

Reimbursable Method

Public employers and nonprofit organizations described under section 501(c)(3) of the Internal Revenue Code have the option of becoming reimbursable employers. Employers electing the reimbursable method, also known as the cost-of-benefits method, are required to reimburse the UI Fund on a dollar-for-dollar basis for all benefits paid to their former employees and charged to their account. Reimbursable employers are billed quarterly, and payment is due within 30 days of the statement date.

For public employers, financing under the reimbursable method must remain in effect for two complete calendar years. For nonprofit employers, financing under the reimbursable method must remain in effect for five complete calendar years. Employers who terminate their reimbursable coverage remain liable for UI benefits paid to their former employees covered under this program for a period of three calendar years.

For a detailed explanation of the reimbursable method, refer to *Information Sheet: Nonprofit and/or Public Entities* (DE 231NP) (PDF) and *Potential Liability for Unemployment Insurance (UI) Benefits When Electing the Reimbursable Method of Financing Under the California Unemployment Insurance Code (CUIC)* (DE 1378F) (PDF). To obtain these publications, visit Forms and Publications (edd.ca.gov/payroll_taxes/forms_and_publications.htm) or contact the Taxpayer Assistance Center at 1-888-745-3886. For additional information, contact:

Employment Development Department
Reimbursable Accounting Group, MIC 19
PO Box 826880
Sacramento, CA 94280-0001

Phone: 1-916-653-5846

School Employees Fund Method

California public school districts, kindergarten through 12th grade, California community colleges, and charter schools may elect to participate in the School Employees Fund (SEF), which is a special UI reimbursable financing method available for school districts. For additional information, visit SEF (edd.ca.gov/en/Payroll_Taxes/School_Employees_Fund) or contact the SEF Unit at 1-916-653-5380.

How Your UI Tax Rate Is Determined

Tax Rate Schedules

The UI tax rates are based on one of seven tax rate schedules, AA through F, established by law. The first step in the annual process of establishing the UI tax rates for the calendar year is for the EDD to determine which of the seven tax rate schedules will be in effect. Employers are assigned their UI tax rates from the same rate schedule.

New Employer – UI Tax Rate and Reserve Account

A UI reserve account is a nonmonetary account that is set up when an employer registers with the EDD. New employers are assigned a 3.4 percent (.034) UI contribution rate for a period of two to three years. This will depend on when the employer meets the criteria under section 982(b) of the California Unemployment Insurance Code (CUIC). After that, an employer's UI contribution rate is determined by their experience rating and the condition of the UI Fund.

Notice of Tax Rates

Each December, the Employment Development Department (EDD) mails the *Notice of Contribution Rates and Statement of UI Reserve Account* (DE 2088) that shows your Unemployment Insurance (UI), and Employment Training Tax (ETT) tax rates and taxable wage limits for the upcoming year. For SDI rate information visit Tax-Rated Employers (edd.ca.gov/tax-rated-employers). If you have address changes or agent updates, contact the EDD immediately in order to receive your notice timely.

You may protest any item on the DE 2088 except SDI and ETT, which are specifically set by law. To protest online, visit the EDD e-Services for Business (edd.ca.gov/eServices). You must provide a valid Letter ID with the associated tax rate year you are protesting within 60 days of the issued date on the notice. You may also file a protest in writing which must be postmarked within 60 days of the issued date on the notice. Include your employer payroll tax account number, the specific items you wish to protest, and the reason you are protesting. An extension of up to 60 days may be granted for *good cause* if your request is submitted before the protest deadline.

For more information about the DE 2088 or protest information, review the *Explanation of the Notice of Contribution Rates and Statement of UI Reserve Account (DE 2088) for the Period Shown on Your DE 2088* (DE 2088C) (PDF) (edd.ca.gov/pdf_pub_ctr/de2088c.pdf) or contact the Taxpayer Assistance Center at 1-888-745-3886.

Federal Unemployment Tax Act Certification

The Internal Revenue Service (IRS) uses the Federal Unemployment Tax Act (FUTA) certification process to verify that the total taxable wages claimed on the *Employer's Annual Federal Unemployment (FUTA) Tax Return* (Form 940) or the federal *Household Employment Taxes* (Form 1040, Schedule H) was actually paid to the state. Under this **dual** system, you are subject to both the state and federal payroll tax requirements.

You are required to file reports and pay UI taxes with the EDD. You are also required to file a Form 940 with IRS to report total taxable UI wages and pay any federal Unemployment Tax due. Generally, you can take a federal credit against your FUTA tax for the UI taxes you paid to California. You may request a FUTA Recertification at Ask EDD (askedd.edd.ca.gov) and follow the prompts under Payroll Tax.

On an annual basis, the IRS and the EDD compare amounts reported on your IRS Form 940 to the Total Subject Wages (line C) and UI Taxable Wages (line D2) reported on your EDD *Quarterly Contribution Return and Report of Wages* (DE 9). When an *out-of-balance* condition exists, reconciliation must be made or an assessment may be issued by either the IRS or the EDD. A common reason for an *out-of-balance* is a change of entity or federal employer identification number (FEIN) that has not been updated with the EDD. You can view or update your FEIN and make changes to your account at e-Services for Business (edd.ca.gov/eServices). For more FUTA information, visit the FUTA Information page (edd.ca.gov/en/payroll_taxes/federal-unemployment-tax-act) or contact the EDD FUTA Certification Unit at 1-916-654-8545.

Reserve Account Transfers

When an employer acquires all or part of an ongoing business and continues to operate the business without substantial reduction of personnel resulting from the acquisition, the employer may request the previous owner's UI reserve account balance transferred to the new ownership by completing an *Application for Transfer of Reserve Account* (DE 4453). This form can be filed electronically through e-Services for Business (edd.ca.gov/eServices). If the EDD approves the transfer, the UI tax rate will be recalculated and may result in an immediate reduction or increase in the UI tax rate. For further information regarding reserve account transfers, call 1-916-653-7795.

Note:

- When a UI reserve account transfer is approved, the employer requesting the transfer will receive a revised DE 2088 stating the UI tax rate.
- Employers who receive a reserve account transfer accept responsibility for the UI benefit charges for the previous owner's former employees. This may increase your UI tax rate in future years.
- A reserve account transfer cannot be reversed once it has been completed.
- There are time limits to qualify for a reserve account transfer. Apply for a reserve account transfer immediately after purchasing an ongoing business.

Wages in Another State

Section 930.1 of the California Unemployment Insurance Code (CUIC) provides that a California employer who pays wages to an employee for employment subject to the unemployment insurance laws of another state, and reports to that state, can use such wages in computing the UI taxable wage limit in the same calendar year if the individual is subsequently transferred to California. Such wages may not be used to arrive at the taxable wage limit for State Disability Insurance purposes.

Interstate Reciprocal Coverage Elections for Multistate Workers

When an individual performs services in two or more states and the services are not localized in any one state, under the provisions of CUIC (sections 602 and 603), the employer may request to report the individual's services to one state.

Upon approval for UI and State Disability Insurance purposes, the employer may report to any state in which (a) services are performed, (b) the employee has residence, or (c) the employer maintains a place of business.

Note: Special reporting may be required for California Personal Income Tax withholding purposes.

For additional information, refer to the _Information Sheet: Multistate Employment (DE 231D) (PDF)_ (edd.ca.gov/pdf_pub_ctr/de231d.pdf) or contact the Taxpayer Assistance Center at 1-888-745-3886.

Tips for Reducing Your UI Tax Rate

UI tax works like any other insurance premium. An employer may pay a lower rate when former employees make fewer claims on the employer's payroll tax account. The following steps may help reduce your UI tax rate:

- Maintain a stable workforce; it could save you UI taxes. High employee turnover increases the potential of benefits charged to your reserve account.
- Submit your _Payroll Tax Deposit_ (DE 88) within the required time limits to ensure your UI contributions are included in calculating your UI tax rate for the following year.
- Respond timely to the _Benefit Audit_ (DE 1296B, DE 1296NER, and DE 1296NBA). It may lead to the reversal of related charges to your reserve or reimbursable account. For additional information, refer to Benefit Audits to Determine Fraud on page 90.
- Respond timely to the _Notice of Unemployment Insurance Claim Filed_ (DE 1101CZ or DE 1101ER) if you believe that a former employee does not meet the UI eligibility criteria. A timely response to a DE 1101CZ or DE 1101ER may reduce charges to your reserve account. For added convenience, employers and third-party administrators can elect to electronically receive and respond to the DE 1101CZ through the State Information Data Exchange System (SIDES). Visit SIDES (edd.ca.gov/SIDES) to learn more.
- Respond timely to the _Notice of Wages Used for Unemployment Insurance (UI) Claim_ (DE 1545) if you believe the wages used to establish a claim are incorrect, the employee is still working, or if you believe a former employee does not meet the UI eligibility criteria. A timely response to a DE 1545 may reduce charges to your reserve account.
- Conduct and document an exit interview to help you to understand why the employee is leaving. This may result in changes to your policies or procedures that will assist you in retaining your employees. Written documentation of the exit interview may be important in supporting your protest.
- Permit leaves of absence because they may help keep fully trained personnel.
- Keep good personnel records to justify any actions taken. Give written warnings prior to discharging an employee and keep a copy of these warnings and other supporting information. For more information, refer to the Recordkeeping section on page 77.
- Protest UI benefit claims for former employees who you believe are not eligible for benefits (for example, employee voluntarily quit or was discharged for misconduct, etc.). Answer UI claim notices promptly, accurately, and in detail.
- Rehire former employees who are currently receiving UI benefits that may be charged against your reserve account.
- Report refusals of work to the EDD at AskEDD (askedd.edd.ca.gov) and follow the prompts under Unemployment Insurance Benefits.
- Provide clear, specific answers to phone interview questions from EDD personnel.
- Review your _Statement of Charges to Reserve Account_ (DE 428T) and report inaccuracies within the protest time limits.
- Bring witnesses with firsthand knowledge of pertinent facts when attending an appeal hearing.

For additional information on the UI program or assistance in reducing UI costs, refer to the booklet _Managing Unemployment Insurance Costs (DE 4527) (PDF)_ (edd.ca.gov/pdf_pub_ctr/de4527.pdf).

Fraud Prevention, Detection, and Reporting

The Employment Development Department (EDD) recognizes your concerns about imposter fraud and the threat of identity theft. Imposter fraud and identity theft occurs when someone steals your employees' employment or personal information and uses that information for personal gain. We actively investigate cases of imposter fraud and are committed to taking the steps necessary to protect the integrity of the Unemployment Insurance (UI) Fund. To assist in these efforts, you may receive a *Request for Additional Information* (DE 1326ER) asking you to validate information provided to us by an individual when we suspect a UI claim may have potential identity or imposter issues. Completing and returning the DE 1326ER with the requested information will assist us in resolving these issues promptly. For more information, visit our fraud detection and prevention activities (edd.ca.gov/en/Unemployment/Responding_to_UI_Claim_Notices).

We also encourage you to take all necessary steps to protect your employees' Social Security numbers (SSN) and other identifying information. A key way to protect yourself and your employees is by properly disposing of your old payroll records. California law requires you to properly destroy (for example, shred, erase, etc.) the personal information on all records under your control. Your employees may sue you for civil damages if you fail to protect their confidential information. For more information on California privacy legislation and protecting yourself and your employees from identity theft, visit the Office of Privacy Protection (oag.ca.gov/privacy).

To minimize potential fraud and protect your UI reserve account, we urge you to carefully review each EDD statement and notice and respond as directed in a timely manner to any items for which you have questions. If you suspect your payroll or personnel data has been compromised, report the incident immediately to our Fraud Hotline at 1-800-229-6297 or by submitting a fraud reporting form (edd.ca.gov/en/about_edd/fraud/).

Additionally, the Social Security Administration (SSA) offers employers and authorized agents a service for verifying employees' SSNs. For information on how to access the SSA's SSN verification service, visit the SSA (ssa.gov/employer/ssnv.htm) or contact your local SSA office.

To learn about steps that you can take to fight imposter fraud, protect your employees, and control your UI costs, review the brochure How You Can Prevent Unemployment Insurance Imposter Fraud (DE 2360ER) (PDF) (edd.ca.gov/pdf_pub_ctr/de2360er.pdf).

UI Rate Manipulation

There are several types of schemes businesses use to unlawfully lower their UI contribution rates. These UI rate manipulation schemes typically involve a business with a high UI tax rate obtaining a lower UI rate through the creation of a new corporate entity or through the purchase of a shell business with a low UI rate. The practice of UI rate manipulation threatens the stability of California's UI Fund and creates an unfair advantage for those businesses that use these schemes to lower their rates.

In 2005, California implemented a law to prevent UI rate manipulation; it requires employers who are illegally lowering their UI rates to pay at the highest rate provided by law plus an additional 2 percent. The law also provides for the greater of a $5,000 penalty or 10 percent of underreported contributions, penalty, or interest for anyone knowingly advising another person or business to violate California's UI rate and reporting laws.

This law also made changes regarding the transfer of UI reserve account balances and specified that whenever a business transferred all or part of its business or payroll to another employer, the reserve account attributable to the transferred business will also be transferred if they are under common ownership, management, or control. It also provides that the transfer will be denied if the acquisition was for the purpose of obtaining a lower UI rate.

For more information, visit UI rate manipulation (edd.ca.gov/payroll_taxes/suta_dumping.htm) or contact the Taxpayer Assistance Center at 1-888-745-3886. If outside the U.S. or Canada, call 1-916-464-3502.

Go Paperless!
You can view or download this guide at California Employer Guides
(edd.ca.gov/en/Payroll_Taxes/Employers_Guides).

Unemployment Insurance Funding

The California Unemployment Insurance (UI) program is funded through payroll taxes paid by employers. These taxes are placed in the UI Fund and benefits are paid to qualified claimants from this fund. The individual tax reserve account established for each employer has no monetary value. The reserve account is an accounting tool used to keep track of credits and charges made against the employer's account to determine their annual UI tax rate. For additional information, refer to *Unemployment Insurance Taxes* on page 80.

Benefit Amount

The maximum amount of UI benefits payable to a claimant during a regular benefit year is 26 times the claimant's weekly benefit amount or one-half of the total base period earnings, whichever is less. The benefit year is a 52-week period starting on the effective date of a new UI claim. The base period consists of four calendar quarters of three months each. When a base period begins and which calendar quarters are used depends on the date the claim begins and whether the claim is for UI or for Disability Insurance (DI).

For UI, there are two types of base periods that may be used to establish a claim: the Standard Base Period (SBP) and the Alternate Base Period (ABP). The SBP is the **first** four of the last five completed calendar quarters prior to the beginning date of the UI claim. If a claimant does not have sufficient wages in the SBP to establish a claim, the Employment Development Department (EDD) will consider whether the claimant qualifies to file a claim using the ABP. The ABP is the four most recently completed calendar quarters prior to the beginning date of the claim. The ABP can **only** be used to file a UI claim when there are not enough wages earned in the SBP to file a monetarily valid UI claim. Refer to page 92 for more information about the ABP.

Current Weekly UI Benefit Amount			Maximum Charged to Reserve Account
Year	Minimum	Maximum	for Each Employee for a Regular Claim
2024	$40	$450	$11,700
2023	$40	$450	$11,700

Benefit Qualifications

To be eligible for UI benefits, claimants must:

- Be unemployed through no fault of their own.
- Be totally or partially unemployed and registered for work with the EDD as required.
- Accurately report all earnings during their weekly claim certification – even those from part-time or temporary work.
- Be physically **able to work** in their usual occupation or in other work for which they are reasonably qualified.
- Be **available for work** by being ready and willing to immediately accept suitable work in their usual occupation or in an occupation for which they are reasonably qualified.
- Be actively **seeking work** on their own behalf.
- Have received a minimum amount of wages during the base period. For additional information, refer to the *Qualifying UI Wages* section on page 85.
- Comply with regulations in regard to filing claims.

Once a claim is filed, EDD staff will determine if there are eligibility issues. An EDD representative may call employers as well as claimants to resolve eligibility issues.

A claimant may be ineligible for UI benefits if the claimant:

- Was discharged for misconduct connected to their work, proof of misconduct rests with the employer.
- Voluntarily quit without good cause, includes quitting for personal reasons, to go to school, or to move.
- Files a UI claim during a recess period, if they worked for a school employer, and had reasonable assurance of returning to work for a school employer.
- Refused suitable work without good cause.
- Failed to take part in reemployment services.
- Failed to apply for a job when referred by a public employment office.
- Failed to make reasonable efforts to look for work.
- Failed to comply with regulations.
- Made false statements or withheld information for the purpose of receiving UI benefits.
- Is not legally entitled to work in the U.S.
- Is not able to work or is not available for work.
- Is working full-time or earns wages totaling more than 25 percent of their weekly UI benefit amount.
- Voluntarily left work due to a trade dispute.

Certain types of employees are not covered for UI benefits. For additional information, refer to:

- *Information Sheet: Types of Employment* (DE 231TE).
- *Information Sheet: Types of Payments* (DE 231TP).

The DE 231TE and DE 231TP are available at Forms and Publications (edd.ca.gov/payroll_taxes/forms_and_publications.htm).

Qualifying UI Wages

To have a valid UI claim, individuals must have earned:

- $1,300 or more in covered employment wages in one quarter of the base period, or
- $900 or more in covered employment wages in the base period quarter with the highest earnings and earned at least 1.25 times the high quarter earnings during the entire base period.

Certain types of payments made to employees are not considered covered employment wages for UI purposes. For additional information, refer to *Information Sheet: Types of Payments* (DE 231TP) (PDF) (edd.ca.gov/pdf_pub_ctr/de231tp.pdf). The table shows if certain types of jobs and types of income are taxable for UI. If the table shows that a job or type of income is **not subject** to UI tax, then that income is excluded from establishing a UI claim.

UI Eligibility Determination

The EDD schedules fact-finding phone interviews or sends questionnaires when there are eligibility questions regarding a claim. Our staff will talk to the claimant, employer, and appropriate third parties as necessary to make a decision. Based on the decision, benefits will either be paid or denied. If benefits are denied, a notice will be issued to the claimant. If the employer responds timely to the first notice sent by the EDD and addresses the issue being decided, a notice will also be sent to the employer.

Note: The maximum amount an employer can be charged on a regular claim is $11,700. Refer to Benefit Amount on page 84. In addition, an employer's reserve account may be subject to charges for benefits paid on a Training Extension (TE) claim. Claimants who have been approved for California Training Benefits, a program established to retain displaced workers who need new skills to return to work, may be eligible for a TE claim. A claimant with a TE claim is eligible to receive a maximum of 52 times their weekly benefit amount on the regular claim, which includes the maximum benefit award of the regular claim.

How to Designate an Agent or Single Address

Tax-Rated Employers or Reimbursable Employers

Tax-Rated or Reimbursable Employers may make address changes or designate an agent by contacting the EDD Tax Branch. Refer to *Changes to Your Business Status* information on page 70.

Reimbursable Employers

Public entity and nonprofit employers should also submit the single agent address or agent information to the EDD Tax Branch to have the address on file changed. To have the *Notice of Unemployment Insurance Claim Filed* (DE 1101CZ) and tax forms sent to the designated single address, refer to *Changes to Your Business Status* information on page 70.

In addition, public entity and nonprofit employers and their agents must elect to have the notice of new or additional claim (DE 1101CZ or DE 1101ER) sent to a designated single address, per section 806 of the California Unemployment Insurance Code.

Send requests for designation of a single address to:

Employment Development Department
Unemployment Insurance Division, MIC 40
PO Box 826880
Sacramento, CA 94280-0001

Fax: 1-916-654-8117

How to Request an Electronic DE 1545

Employers and their agents may electronically obtain the *Notice of Wages Used for Unemployment Insurance (UI) Claim* (DE 1545) through the Electronic Data Interchange (EDI). To obtain information about EDI, contact:

Employment Development Department
Employer Assistance Unit, MIC 16
PO Box 826880
Sacramento, CA 94280-0001

Phone: 1-916-464-2325

Responding to Notices

You need to respond timely and in writing to the *Notice of Unemployment Insurance Claim Filed* (DE 1101CZ or DE 1101ER), *Notice of Wages Used for Unemployment Insurance (UI) Claim* (DE 1545), or the *Notice of Potential Increased Liability for Training Extension Benefits* (DE 1545TE) if:

- The claimant was terminated or voluntarily quit.
- You have knowledge of information that might affect the claimant's eligibility for UI benefits.
- The claimant's name and Social Security number are not correct.
- You want a written decision of eligibility that provides your appeal rights to the EDD's decision.
- The claimant's work was in non-covered employment for UI purposes and the wages should not be used to establish a UI claim, including work performed as an elected official.

If you believe the claimant is not entitled to benefits, it is important to protest in writing when you receive the first notice and within the protest time limits. Refer to page 87 for the Claim Notices and Protest Time Limits table. Your response must include any facts that may affect the claimant's eligibility for UI benefits or the potential liability of your UI reserve account for benefits paid to the claimant.

Protests to the DE 1101CZ, DE 1101ER, DE 1545, DE 1545R, or DE 1545TE should be in writing and mailed to the address noted on the form within the protest time limits of that form. Employers and third-party administrators can elect to electronically receive and respond to the EDD's *Notice of Unemployment Insurance Claim Filed* (DE 1101CZ) using SIDES (edd.ca.gov/SIDES). Protests may be written on the notice or included in a separate letter and should contain the following information:

- Employer's payroll tax account number, name, and address.
- Claimant's name and Social Security number.
- Beginning date of the claim.
- Date of separation from employment.
- Dates of separations and rehires during and following the quarters shown on the DE 1545.
- Information supporting your belief of the claimant's ineligibility. Refer to page 84 for a list of disqualifying events. Protests should include specific facts and circumstances. General statements (for example, employee was fired for misconduct) should be supported with specific events and documentation. This will result in better eligibility decisions based on the facts.
- If the wage information listed on the DE 1545 or DE 1545TE is incorrect, inform the EDD in writing at:

  Employment Development Department
  Employers Assistance Unit, MIC 16
  PO Box 826880
  Sacramento, CA 94280-0001

  Include the following information with your correction of wage information:
  - Employer's payroll tax account number, name, and address.
  - Claimant's name and Social Security number.
  - Beginning date of the claim.
  - Correction to the wage information. Please provide supporting documentation to the correction, such as a copy of the *Quarterly Contribution Return and Report of Wages (Continuation)* (DE 9C) or *Quarterly Contribution and Wage Adjustment Form* (DE 9ADJ).
  - Name, signature, and phone number of the employer or employer representative preparing the wage correction.
  - Date of the wage correction.
- The protest should be signed by the person having personal knowledge of the facts or having access to records containing the facts.

Note: If a written protest is not submitted, or submitted untimely for the DE 1101CZ, DE 1101ER, DE 1545, or DE 1545TE, you waive your right to protest your UI reserve account's potential liability for benefits paid to the claimant and your right to appeal the EDD determination.

Subsequent Benefit Year

If you receive a notice that a subsequent benefit year has been established, you must resubmit any facts you furnished on the initial *Notice of Unemployment Insurance Claim Filed* (DE 1101CZ or DE 1101ER) to be entitled to a determination or ruling based on such facts for the later benefit year.

Claim Notices and Protest Time Limits	
Notice	**Postmarked Within**
DE 1101CZ or DE 1101ER Mailed to the last employer when a current or former employee files a new UI claim or an existing claim is reopened.	10 calendar days of the date mailed to you. The date is printed on the top right side of the DE 1101CZ and the DE 1101ER.
DE 1545 Issued to all base period employers after a claimant receives the first UI payment. This notice informs each employer of the wages used to establish the claim and the amount of potential charges to their UI reserve account for that claim. **Note:** Employers and their agents may obtain the DE 1545 electronically. Refer to How to Request an Electronic DE 1545 on <u>page 86</u>.	The deadline to submit a ruling request is located on the top right side of the DE 1545. To request a ruling, submit separation information within 15 calendar days from the mail date. If wage information is incorrect, submit the information within 30 calendar days.
DE 1545TE Mailed to base period employers only when a former employee has been approved for the California Training Benefits (CTB) program. This form will inform you of the maximum amount of potential benefits payable, including training extension benefits, and the amount of potential charges to your UI reserve account. When protesting a former employee's eligibility for the CTB program, employers should address the particular criteria that individuals must meet under section 1269 and 1269.1 of the California Unemployment Insurance Code.	15 calendar days from the mail date.

Note: If you respond untimely, provide the reason you are submitting the eligibility information untimely and the EDD will determine if you had **good cause** for not submitting your response timely. If there is a finding of **good cause**, you will be entitled to receive a notice of determination or ruling. If it is determined that you did not have *good cause* for the late response, a *Response to Employer Communication* (DE 4614) will be issued. This form can be appealed if you disagree with the determination. Also, if you respond untimely with eligibility information, the EDD will conduct a determination of eligibility with the claimant regardless of whether you are entitled to a notice of determination or ruling.

For the latest tax news and employer resources, visit
<u>California Employer News and Updates</u>
(edd.ca.gov/payroll_taxes/employer-news.htm).

Subscribe to the EDD no-cost <u>email subscription services</u>
(edd.ca.gov/about_edd/get_email_notices.htm).

Unemployment Insurance Benefits

Notices of Determination, Ruling, or Modification

You will receive one of the following DE 1080 notices in response to eligibility issues you reported on the *Notice of Unemployment Insurance Claim Filed* (DE 1101CZ or DE 1101ER), *Notice of Wages Used for Unemployment Insurance (UI) Claim* (DE 1545), or the *Notice of Potential Increased Liability for Training Extension Benefits* (DE 1545TE).

Notice	Purpose
DE 1080CZ: • *Notice of Determination*	**Reimbursable Employers** Sent to an employer who responds timely to a DE 1101CZ or DE 1101ER, and who submits information about quits and discharges. The notice informs the employer whether or not the claimant was found eligible for Unemployment Insurance (UI) benefits. **Tax-rated and Reimbursable Employers** Sent to an employer who responds timely to a DE 1101CZ, DE 1101ER, DE 1545, or DE 1545TE, or who provides eligibility information about issues other than quits or discharges that can affect a claimant's eligibility for UI benefits, such as job refusals or a claimant's unavailability for work because of school attendance, lack of child care, etc. The notice informs the employer whether or not the claimant was found eligible to receive UI benefits. Refer to page 84 for a list of disqualifying events.
• *Notice of Determination/Ruling*	Sent to a tax-rated employer who responds timely to a DE 1101CZ or DE 1101ER with eligibility information regarding a voluntary quit or discharge. The ruling portion of this notice informs the employer whether or not the reserve account will be charged for UI benefits paid.
• *Notice of Ruling*	Sent to a tax-rated employer who responds timely to a DE 1545 with separation information. The separation must have occurred during or after the base period of the claim. This notice informs the employer whether or not the reserve account will be charged for UI benefits paid.
DE 1080M: • *Notice of Modification*	Sent to the employer who previously received a DE 1080EZ stating that the claimant was disqualified. This form informs the employer that the claimant's disqualification period is over. This notice does not change the original ruling issued to the employer.

Note: Employers who finance UI coverage under one of the reimbursable financing methods receive Notices of Determination, but do not receive Notices of Ruling because they do not have a UI reserve account.

The *Notice of Potential Increased Liability for Training Extension Benefits* (DE 1545TE) provides base-period employers with a timely notice of maximum amount of potential UI benefits, including training extension benefits that may be charged to their accounts. This form is mailed to base-period employers only when a former employee has been approved for the California Training Benefits (CTB) program. When protesting a claimant's eligibility for the CTB program, employers should address the particular criteria that individuals must meet under sections 1269 and 1269.1 of the CUIC.

Unemployment Insurance Benefits

Go Paperless!
You can view or download this guide at California Employer Guides
(edd.ca.gov/en/Payroll_Taxes/Employers_Guides).

Unemployment Insurance Benefits – Appeal Rights

You have the right to file an appeal if you do not agree with a decision made by the Employment Development Department (EDD) about your:

- Former employee's right to receive UI benefits.

- UI reserve account being charged for benefits paid to a former employee.

You must send your written appeal to the EDD **within 30 calendar days of the date the decision was mailed** to you. The EDD will send you an acknowledgement of receipt and registration of your appeal with the phone number for the Office of Appeal hearing the case. The Office of Appeal will schedule a hearing with an Administrative Law Judge (ALJ). Both you and your former employee will be notified of the date, time, and place of the hearing at least 10 days before the hearing date. If you are filing an appeal to a *Notice of Ruling* (DE 1080CZ), the employee is not considered a party to the proceeding and is not notified of the hearing. The ALJ will conduct a hearing and give all interested parties the opportunity to present their evidence. The ALJ will consider the facts presented at the hearing and issue a written decision that is mailed to all concerned parties.

If you do not agree with the ALJ's decision, you may appeal to the California Unemployment Insurance Appeals Board (CUIAB). The CUIAB reviews appeals to decisions rendered by the ALJ. Both the CUIAB and the ALJs operate impartially and independently of the EDD.

The CUIAB provides the following publications to assist in filing an appeal and preparing for an administrative hearing:

- *Appeals Procedure* (DE 1433)

- *Office of Appeals Tax Hearing Information Pamphlet* (DE 6412TF)

For copies of these publications, write to the California Unemployment Insurance Appeals Board at the address shown on the following page. You may also download these forms from CUIAB (cuiab.ca.gov). If you have any questions about filing an appeal, please contact the EDD at 1-800-300-5616.

Note: An EDD *Appeal Form (DE 1000M) (PDF)* (edd.ca.gov/pdf_pub_ctr/de1000m.pdf) is enclosed with all DE 1080s.

For the latest tax news and employer resources, visit
California Employer News and Updates
(edd.ca.gov/payroll_taxes/employer-news.htm).

Subscribe to the EDD no-cost email subscription services
(edd.ca.gov/about_edd/get_email_notices.htm).

False Statement Penalty

Section 1142(a) of the CUIC provides that an employer or the employer's agent may be assessed a cash penalty from 2 to 10 times the claimant's weekly benefit amount if it is determined that the employer, employer's representative, employer's officer, or employer's agent willfully made a false statement or misrepresentation or failed to report a material fact concerning the claimant's termination of employment.

Section 1142(b) of the CUIC provides that an employer or the employer's agent may be assessed a cash penalty from 2 to 10 times the claimant's weekly benefit amount if it is determined that the employer, employer's representative, employer's officer, or employer's agent willfully made a false statement or representation or willfully fails to report a material fact concerning the claimant's reasonable assurance of reemployment as defined in section 1253.3 of the CUIC.

Section 1142.1 of the CUIC provides that an employer may be assessed a cash penalty from 2 to 10 times the claimant's weekly benefit amount if it is determined that the employer, employer representative, employer officer, or employer agent, where the claimant was performing services for an educational institution as defined in section 1253.3, willfully makes a false statement or representation or fails to report a material fact concerning the claimant's termination of employment or regarding any week during which services were performed (as provided in section 1253.3) or any time granted to the claimant for professional development while working for that employer.

If you are not in agreement with the *Notice of Determination or Assessment Under UI Code Section 1142(A)* (DE 3807 SEP) or *Notice of Determination or Assessment Under UI Code Section 1142(B)* (DE 3807 RA), you may file a Petition for Reassessment to an Administrative Law Judge (ALJ), of the California Unemployment Insurance Appeals Board (CUIAB), refer to the *Notice of Petition Rights* (DE 2350). The CUIAB, established separate and apart from the EDD, reviews, hears, and renders impartial and independent decisions in tax and benefit matters related to the CUIC.

Prepare an original and a copy of the petition. The petition may be informal but must be in writing and should:

- Show your EDD employer payroll tax account number and the date of the assessment. For faster processing, enclose a copy of the DE 3807 SEP or DE 3807 RA with your petition.

- Provide the claimant's name and Social Security number.

- Clearly indicate that it is a Petition for Reassessment.

- Describe the reason for the petition and specify the facts or grounds for requesting a reassessment.

- Be signed by you or your authorized agent.

- State your address or that of your agent, if any.

To be timely, the petition must be mailed or delivered to the office shown below within 30 calendar days from the date of assessment. The time to protest can be extended by an ALJ for not more than 30 days but only if **good cause** for the delay is shown. Mail or deliver the original and a copy of your petition for reassessment to:

California Unemployment Insurance Appeals Board
Sacramento Office of Appeals
2400 Venture Oaks Way, Suite 100
Sacramento, CA 95833-4224

Benefit Audits to Determine Fraud

The benefit audit process leads to the recovery of improper UI benefit payments and the potential reversal of related charges to the employer's reserve account when the EDD determines that the claimant was not entitled to UI benefits. The EDD has several processes to detect and deter fraud; thereby, protecting the integrity of the UI program. The *Benefit Audit* (DE 1296B) identifies individuals who may have improperly received UI benefits for weeks in which they worked and had earnings. Each quarter, as part of the EDD fraud detection efforts, DE 1296B audit forms are mailed to employers to request wage information for specific weeks that their California employees may have worked.

Each quarter, the EDD also runs a cross-match with other states' wage records. If it appears an individual may have worked in another state while receiving California UI benefits, then an *Interstate Unemployment Insurance Benefit Payment Audit* (IB 8605) form will be sent to out-of-state employers.

Benefit Audits to Determine Fraud continued

Additionally, as part of our continuing efforts to detect and deter fraud, the EDD cross-matches the Social Security number and start-of-work date (SWD) on a daily basis from the New Employee Registry information reported by employers with UI benefit payment information. An accurate SWD, not the hire date, is important for this cross-match process. If a match is identified, a *New Employee Registry Benefit Audit* (DE 1296NER) audit form will be sent to the employer requesting earnings and eligibility information. The returned employer information is used to identify benefit overpayments and to recover the improper benefit payments.

The DE 1296NER audit form enables the EDD to detect fraud up to six months sooner than the quarterly Benefit Audit Process and protects the UI Fund by reducing overpayments. Employers who have responded to the DE 1296NER audit form will not receive a DE 1296B for the same employee for the same quarter.

Similar to the NER cross-match, the EDD runs the National Directory of New Hires (NDNH) cross-match on a weekly basis which identifies work earnings with employers in other states. When the NDNH cross-match identifies an overlap between the SWD reported by the employer and weeks the claimant certified for UI benefits, a *New Hire Benefit Audit* (DE 1296NBA) form is mailed to the employer.

Employers are required by state and federal laws to respond to the DE 1296B, the DE 1296NER, the IB 8605, and the DE 1296NBA benefit audits. Employers' participation in these processes is essential to detect potential fraud and to protect the integrity of the UI program.

Send questions or comments about the benefit audit process to:

Employment Development Department
PO Box 3038, MIC 16A
Sacramento, CA 95812-3038

Phone: 1-866-401-2849

For more information visit <u>Benefit Fraud</u> (edd.ca.gov/Unemployment/Completing_Benefit_Audit_Forms.htm).

Back Pay Award

Employees who receive UI benefits and later receive back pay awards or settlements must have the Back Pay Award or settlement allocated to the period for which it was awarded. The EDD must be reimbursed an amount that equals the amount of UI benefits received if the Back Pay Award covers the same period for which UI benefits were paid. Back pay is considered wages and should be reported within 30 days from the settlement or agreement date.

A determination must be made regarding who is responsible to repay the EDD for the overpaid benefit amounts. If the Back Pay Award agreement states that the employer will withhold overpayment amounts from the Back Pay Award or settlement, the employer is responsible for submitting the amounts withheld to the EDD to clear the overpayment. The employer must provide the claimant's name and complete Social Security number and information concerning the period covered by the Back Pay Award.

At the employer's request, the EDD will determine the amount of UI benefits to be repaid, establish an overpayment, and notify the claimant and employer. *Employer* refers to both tax-rated and reimbursable employers. Reimbursable employers will receive credits against their future charges only after the liability has been paid. For further information, contact:

Employment Development Department UI Overpayment Center, #017
PO Box 1043
Atwood, CA 92811-1044

Phone: 1-714-687-4400

Workers' Compensation Benefits

Employees who received UI benefits and later receive workers' compensation benefits in the form of Temporary Total Disability (TTD) benefits, Vocational Rehabilitation Maintenance Allowance (VRMA), or settlements for the same period must repay the EDD an amount equal to the UI benefits received. For further information, contact:

Employment Development Department
Workers' Compensation Specialist
PO Box 2588
Rancho Cordova, CA 95670

Phone: 1-916-464-0713

Statement of Charges

Each September, the annual *Statement of Charges to Reserve Account* (DE 428T) is mailed to you. This statement notifies you of the Unemployment Insurance (UI) benefit charges and credits to your reserve account from July 1 through June 30 of the previous fiscal year. Charges are itemized and based on the UI benefits paid to your former employees. Charges to your reserve account may increase your UI contribution rate for the next calendar year. It is important to review your statement carefully and respond timely if you do not agree with the charges. To protest online, visit e-Services for Business (edd.ca.gov/eServices). You must provide a valid Letter ID for the period you are protesting within 60 days of the issued date on the notice. File a protest in writing postmarked within 60 days of the issued date on the notice. An extension of up to 60 days may be granted for *good cause* (refer to page 56) if your request is submitted before the protest deadline. When filing your protest, you must include your Employment Development Department (EDD) eight-digit employer payroll tax account number, the claimant's name, Social Security number, claim date, the dollar amount, total number of claimants protested, and the specific reason for protesting. Protests with missing information will be returned.

Protest charges may be submitted online through e-Services for Business or by mail to:

Employment Development Department
Contribution Rate Group
PO Box 826831
Sacramento, CA 94230-6831

For a sample form and detailed instructions on how to file a protest, refer to the *DE 428T Protest Sample Form* (DE 428C) by visiting Payroll Taxes – Forms and Publications (edd.ca.gov/en/payroll_taxes/forms_and_publications) or contact the Taxpayer Assistance Center at 1-888-745-3886.

To ensure your DE 428T is received timely, please make the necessary updates to your address or agent information. For your convenience, these updates can be submitted online using e-Services for Business.

Alternate Base Period

The Alternate Base Period (ABP) program requires the EDD to use more recently earned wages to calculate monetary eligibility for new UI claims for unemployed individuals who do not qualify for a UI claim using the Standard Base Period (SBP). The SBP uses the wages earned in the first four of the last five completed calendar quarters prior to the beginning date of the UI claim. The ABP uses the wages earned in the four most recently completed calendar quarters.

In addition to employers' current quarterly wage reporting, if the ABP wages are not showing in the EDD database, employers will be asked to provide the wages for claimants. At times, employers may be asked to provide wages prior to the quarterly wage reporting. The EDD will only request wages from employers if it appears that claimants have enough wages to qualify for a UI claim using the ABP. If it is necessary for the EDD to obtain the wages from the employer, the EDD will mail the employer a *Request for Wages* (DE 1919) to request wage information for each of the five most recently completed quarters. This will assist the EDD in determining if the claimant qualifies for a claim using the SBP or ABP. Employers have 10 days to respond to the EDD request.

In addition to mailing the employer a DE 1919, the EDD will mail the claimant an *Affidavit of Wages* (DE 23A) to request the wage information. If the employer does not respond to the EDD request for wage information within the 10 days, and the claimant provides the DE 23A along with tangible evidence of the wages earned, the EDD will file the claim based on the wage information provided by the claimant.

If the base period wages on an ABP claim are later adjusted when the quarterly wages are reported by the employer, an overpayment may not be established on the ABP claim unless the claim was based on fraudulent information provided by the claimant. Meaning, if employers do not respond timely to the EDD original DE 1919, they may incur reserve account charges they might not have otherwise incurred.

Layoff Alternatives

Partial UI Claims

The Partial Unemployment Insurance (UI) Claim program enables employers to keep trained employees who are partially employed during slow business periods. Employers may use the Partial UI Claim program if employees are temporarily working reduced hours or have been placed on layoff status for no more than two consecutive weeks. For information about partial claims and the partial forms, refer to the *Notice of Reduced Earnings* (DE 2063) and *Notice of Reduced Earnings (Fisherperson)* (DE 2063F) by visiting Partial Claims FAQs (edd.ca.gov/en/unemployment/partial_claims).

If you participate in the program, you should:

- Instruct your employees to call the EDD UI toll-free numbers to file a UI claim by phone.
- Instruct your employees to advise the EDD they are participating in the Partial UI Claims program.
- Complete the employer portion of the *Notice of Reduced Earnings* (DE 2063) and issue it to your employees.
- Instruct employees to complete and sign the DE 2063 and mail it to the EDD.

If an employee has no wages and does not work for two consecutive weeks, instruct the employee to contact the Employment Development Department (EDD) to obtain the regular *Continued Claim* (DE 4581) form. Participation in this program may increase the employer's UI tax rate.

For more information about partial UI claims, contact one of the toll-free UI phone numbers on page 106 or visit UI Claims (edd.ca.gov/en/unemployment/partial_claims).

Work Sharing Program

The Work Sharing program is available to employers who reduce employee wages and hours as an alternative to a layoff. The affected workforce or work units must consist of two or more employees who comprise at least 10 percent of the workforce or work units and the employer must meet other requirements to participate. The employer must sign a *Work Sharing (WS) Unemployment Insurance Plan Application* (DE 8686) with the EDD and comply with all requirements to remain eligible for participation. The DE 8686 must be periodically renewed. Participation in this program may increase the employer's UI tax rate. If you are interested in participating in the program or would like additional information, visit Work Sharing claims (edd.ca.gov/WorkSharing) or contact:

Employment Development Department
Special Claims Office
PO Box 419076
Rancho Cordova, CA 95741-9076

Phone: 1-916-464-3343
Fax: 1-916-464-2616
Alternate fax: 1-916-464-3333

Note: Employees participating in the Work Sharing or Partial Claims programs cannot use Tele-Cert or the EDD UI Online to certify for UI weekly benefits. Participants of these programs are required to continue using the existing paper continued claim form by mail.

Notice of Layoff

Employers who have employed 75 or more full and part time employees in the preceding 12 months and are planning plant closures, or layoffs of 50 or more employees within a 30-day period, or relocation of at least 100 miles affecting any number of employees, must give affected employees at least 60 days written notice. Employees must have been employed for at least six of the 12 months preceding the date of required notice to be counted. Refer to the *Plant Closure or Mass Layoff* section on page 74 for additional information.

Wages Notices

In the event of a layoff or business closure involving 10 or more employees, the EDD Wages Notice Group will investigate and post Electronic Wages Notices (EWN) for staff in the EDD offices to use. The EWNs contain wage findings (for example, findings on in-lieu-of-notice pay and bonuses) to ensure consistent determinations when several employees may be affected by the same set of facts. For additional information, visit mass layoffs and wage notices (edd.ca.gov/unemployment/mass_layoffs_and_wage_notices.htm).

State Disability Insurance Program

The State Disability Insurance (SDI) program provides Disability Insurance (DI) and Paid Family Leave (PFL) benefits to eligible workers who need to take time off work due to a disability or family leave. DI is a component of the SDI program. DI provides partial wage replacement benefits to eligible California workers who have a loss of wages when they are unable to work due to a non-work-related illness, injury, or pregnancy. PFL is another component of the SDI program. It covers family leave. PFL provides benefits to eligible workers who take time off work to care for a seriously ill child, parent, parent-in-law, grandparent, grandchild, sibling, spouse, or registered domestic partner. Benefits are available to new parents who need time off work to bond with a new child through birth, adoption, or foster care placement. Benefits are also available to eligible workers who take time off work to participate in a qualifying event because of a spouse, registered domestic partner, parent, or child's military deployment to a foreign country.

Taxes – Who Pays for State Disability Insurance?

The SDI program, which includes DI and PFL, is funded through mandatory employee payroll deductions for most California workers. California law requires employers to provide coverage for employees with payroll in excess of $100 in a calendar quarter. There are a few exceptions. Some of those specifically excluded are:
- Some domestic workers.
- Some governmental employees.
- Employees of interstate railroads.
- Employees of some nonprofit agencies.
- Individuals claiming a religious exemption.

The SDI tax rate may be adjusted annually to not more than 1.5 percent (.015) or less than 0.1 percent (.001) depending on the balance in the Disability Fund. Employee contributions withheld are paid by the employer to either the Disability Fund or a Voluntary Plan (refer to page 95).

Employee Benefits

Eligible employees may file for DI benefits for each occurrence of disability or PFL benefits up to the maximum number of weeks allowed within any 12-month period to care, bond or participate in a qualifying event because of a family member's military deployment to a foreign country. The brochure *Disability Insurance Provisions* (DE 2515) contains general information on DI eligibility. The *Paid Family Leave Brochure* (DE 2511) contains general information on PFL eligibility. The *Claim for Disability Insurance (DI) Benefits* (DE 2501) and *Claim for Paid Family Leave (PFL) Benefits* (DE 2501F) are paper forms that contain applications to file for benefits and additional program information. Employees can also apply electronically through SDI Online (edd.ca.gov/disability/sdi_online.htm).

California employers whose employees are subject to SDI contributions must provide new employees the DE 2515 and the DE 2511 and post the Notice to Employees (DE 1857A) poster. The California Unemployment Insurance Code (CUIC) requires employers to provide general DI information to each employee unable to work due to a non-work-related illness, injury, or pregnancy. Employers are also required to provide PFL information to each employee requesting time off to care for a seriously ill family member, to bond with a new child, or to participate in a qualifying event resulting because of family member's military deployment to a foreign country. The brochures and applications are provided to employers at no cost. Additional copies may be ordered at EDD Forms (edd.ca.gov/forms) or contact the Taxpayer Assistance Center at 1-888-745-3886.

Employer Claim Notices

When a DI claim is filed, the employers reported on the DI claim form will receive a *Notice to Employer of Disability Insurance Claim Filed* (DE 2503). When a PFL claim is filed, the employers will receive a *Notice of Paid Family Leave (PFL) Claim Filed* (DE 2503F). Employers are required to complete and return the DE 2503 or DE 2503F within two working days. The DE 2503 can also be submitted electronically using SDI Online (edd.ca.gov/disability/sdi_online.htm).

To deter fraud, respond immediately if you are not the employer shown on the DE 2503 or DE 2503F, or if the individual filing for benefits:
- Is not your employee.
- Has quit their job.
- Is receiving wages.
- Has not stopped working.
- Is known to be working for another employer.

Note: Your Unemployment Insurance reserve account will not be affected when your employees file DI or PFL claims. Because employees pay for DI and PFL through payroll deductions, you will not be notified of claimant employee eligibility for DI and PFL benefits.

State Disability Insurance

SDI Online

SDI Online is an electronic claim filing system available to employers, individuals filing for benefits, physicians or practitioners, Voluntary Plan employers, and third-party administrators for submission of DI and PFL claim information. Employers can securely submit employee information (for example, wages earned, last day worked, etc.) for DI claims online. For additional information, visit SDI Online (edd.ca.gov/en/disability/SDI_Online).

Voluntary Plan

California law allows an employer to apply to the EDD for approval of a Voluntary Plan (VP) for the payment of DI and PFL benefits in place of the mandatory SDI coverage. A VP must provide all the benefits of SDI, at least one benefit that is better than SDI, and it cannot cost employees more than SDI. To be approved for a VP, the employer must post a security deposit with the EDD.

Once a VP is approved, the employer is no longer required to send SDI withholdings to the EDD for those employees covered by the VP. Instead, if the plan is paid by the employees, the employer holds the VP contributions in a trust fund to pay DI or PFL benefit claims and approved expenses. The employer may enlist a greater benefit by paying for the plan rather than having the employees pay for it. The VP employer pays a quarterly assessment to the EDD based on the taxable wages of employees participating in the plan and other factors.

A VP must provide better coverage without additional cost to the employees. Based on claims experience, excess funds may be used to increase benefit levels or lower contributions. Please note that any money collected for VP purposes must be used only for the benefit of employees who contribute to the plan.

An employer considering a VP commitment should be aware that the employer takes ultimate responsibility for the plan benefits and expenses. If the accumulated VP trust fund is inadequate to cover benefits or expenses, the employer is responsible to cover the deficit. The employer may loan or gift the plan: any loans made to the VP may be recovered from future excess VP trust funds. If a plan terminates and there are insufficient trust funds, the employer must assume the financial obligation until all plan liabilities have been met.

For more information on **VP options**, refer to the *Employers' Guide to Voluntary Plan Procedures* (DE 2040) (PDF) (edd.ca.gov/pdf_pub_ctr/de2040.pdf) call 1-916-653-6839 (TTY users dial the California Relay Service 711), or email VPProgram@edd.ca.gov.

Self-Employed Benefits

Any self-employed individual who receives the major part of their income from the trade, business, or occupation in which they are self-employed may elect coverage for themselves. Under provisions in the CUIC, self-employed individuals who are employers, may elect UI and SDI or SDI coverage only for themselves. Self-employed individuals who are not employers, may only elect SDI coverage for themselves.

Self-employed individuals who elect coverage pay at a rate determined by the prior annual combined usage of all participants.

For more information on elective coverage, refer to the *Information Sheet: Elective Coverage for Employers and Self-Employed Individuals* (DE 231EC) (PDF) (edd.ca.gov/pdf_pub_ctr/de231ec.pdf).

For additional information, refer to the *Fact Sheet: Disability Insurance Elective Coverage Program (DIEC)* (DE 8714CC) (PDF) (edd.ca.gov/pdf_pub_ctr/de8714cc.pdf) or call the Taxpayer Assistance Center at 1-888-745-3886.

Workers' Compensation Insurance

Workers' compensation insurance is an employer paid insurance that provides benefits to eligible workers experiencing a loss of wages when they are unable to perform their regular or customary work due to an occupational illness or injury. Generally, employees are not eligible for SDI when receiving workers' compensation benefits unless the SDI rate is greater than the workers' compensation rate. For additional information, visit the Department of Industrial Relations (dir.ca.gov/dwc).

If you have **any** employees, you are required by law to have workers' compensation insurance. Failure to do so is a crime and may result in penalties and closure of your business.

If you have questions about workers' compensation insurance or how to obtain coverage, contact your insurance agent or the Division of Workers' Compensation at 1-800-736-7401.

SDI Fraud

To provide affordable benefits to eligible workers, the SDI program has systems in place to detect and deter fraud. Help fight fraud (edd.ca.gov/about_edd/fraud.htm) by reporting suspected fraudulent activity to the Ask EDD (askedd.edd.ca.gov/AskEDD/s/categorydetails?category=Report_Fraud) fraud reporting form, or contact the Fraud hotline at 1-800-229-6297 or fax 1-866-340-5484.

Employment and Training Services

Workforce Services

The Employment Development Department (EDD) provides a comprehensive range of employment and training services in partnership with state and local agencies through numerous America's Job Center of California℠ (AJCC) locations statewide. The EDD administers several federal employment and training programs, the largest being the Workforce Innovation and Opportunity Act (WIOA) Title I Adult, Dislocated Worker and Youth programs and the Title III Wagner-Peyser Act Employment Service program. These programs provide job seekers with access to employment, education, training, and supportive services to succeed in California's labor market and help match employers with the skilled workers they need to compete in the economy.

Employers may access the following services offered by the WIOA and Wagner-Peyser programs at an AJCC:

- Applicant screenings and referrals
- Recruitment services
- Business closure assistance
- Customized training
- Job placement assistance
- Labor market information
- On-the-job training
- CalJOBS℠

To locate your nearest AJCC, visit the EDD's Office Locator (edd.ca.gov/Office_Locator).

CalJOBS℠

CalJOBS℠ is California's online labor exchange system which provides quick access to a large pool of job-ready candidates. Employers can post job openings, browse resumes, and find qualified candidates for employment.

Employers without internet access or who have special requirements, can be served by customer service representatives who take job opening information by phone or fax, and assist employers in finding qualified applicants. There is no fee to use CalJOBS℠.

To register with CalJOBS℠, you will need your EDD employer payroll tax account number. Visit CalJOBS℠ (caljobs. ca.gov) or call the CalJOBS℠ Employer Help Desk at 1-877-622-4997 for assistance. If you do not have an EDD employer payroll tax account number, refer to page 7 for information about obtaining one.

Visit employment and training services (edd.ca.gov/jobs_and_training/Employer_information.htm) for more information or locate your nearest America's Job Center of California℠ (edd.ca.gov/Office_Locator).

Employment Training Panel

The Employment Training Panel (ETP) is a statewide business-labor training and economic development program. The ETP provides funding to employers to assist in upgrading the skills of their workers through training that leads to good paying, long-term jobs. The ETP was created in 1982 by the California State Legislature and has invested approximately $1.9 billion for the successful training and employment retention of more than 1.5 million workers by over 96,000 California businesses to date. The ETP is a funding agency, not a training agency. Businesses determine their own training needs and how best to provide training.

The ETP funds training to foster job creation and the retention of workers in secure, full-time employment in targeted industries in order to improve California's competitiveness in a global economy and to advance the skills of the state's workforce. The ETP's Core Funding Program primarily funds retraining of currently employed workers in companies threatened by out-of-state competition and has placed special emphasis on training for small businesses with fewer than 100 employees in California.

Funding

The legislature established the Employment Training Tax (ETT) in 1982. All tax-rated employers, including new employers, are subject to the ETT. Employers with positive reserve accounts are assessed 0.1 percent (.001) on the first $7,000 of each employee's wages. Employers do not pay the ETT while their accounts have a negative reserve balance, but they must pay a higher rate of Unemployment Insurance (UI) tax. The maximum ETT collected is $7 per employee, per year. The ETP's Core Funding Program is funded by the ETT. The ETP has also received additional funding for alternative programs. This additional funding has been through partnerships with the California Energy Commission (CEC), as well as through funding from the Labor and Workforce Development Agency (LWDA) to fund specific training programs.

How Is ETP Different?

The ETP's performance-based contracts ensure that ETP funded training results in good-paying, secure jobs. Before an employer may earn training cost reimbursement, trainees must receive a certain number of training hours and must complete the required retention period at their job, depending on the contract type, as well as meet the required ETP minimum wage. The employer determines the training courses, trainers, and types of training that best meet their business needs.

General Information

The ETP contracts directly with tax-rated employers, groups of employers, including associations and chambers of commerce, training agencies, vocational schools, Workforce Development Boards (WDB), and grant recipients under the Workforce Innovation and Opportunity Act (WIOA).

Under its Core Funding Program, the ETP funds the following types of training to promote a healthy labor market in a growing and competitive economy:

- **Retraining** – Helps companies facing out-of-state competition by upgrading the job skills of current employees.

- **New-Hire Training** – Trains unemployed workers eligible to receive California UI benefits or who have exhausted UI benefits within 24 months of the start of training.

- **Special Employment Training (SET)** – The ETP provides limited funding for SET projects to improve the skills and employment security of frontline workers (workers directly producing goods or services) in occupations that pay at least the state average hourly wage. SET projects are not subject to ETP's out-of-state competition requirement, but are a priority for workforce training. SET funding also allows training of frontline workers who earn below the state average, if they are in the following categories:

  o Workers in High Unemployment Areas – Provides training funds for workers in areas where the unemployment rate is significantly higher than the state average.

  o Small Business Skills – Training for small business owners to enhance the competitive position of their business. Owners must have at least one, but no more than nine, full-time employees.

  o Workers with Multiple Barriers to Employment – Training for individuals with barriers to full-time employment, such as, but not limited to, physical disabilities, lack of work history, and limited communication and literacy skills.

  o Seasonal Industries – Training funds for workers employed by companies in seasonal industries.

For more information, including how to apply for funds, eligible entities, training methods, reimbursement rates, and ETP Annual Reports, visit ETP (etp.ca.gov). Interested parties may also contact one of the following ETP offices:

Sacramento Central Office	1-916-327-5640
North Hollywood Regional Office	1-818-755-1313
Sacramento Regional Office	1-916-327-5439
San Diego Regional Office	1-619-881-1777
San Francisco Bay Area Regional Office	1-650-655-6930

Trade Adjustment Assistance

The Trade Adjustment Assistance (TAA) program is a federal program that assists U.S. workers who have lost or may lose their jobs as a result of foreign trade.

The TAA program is administered by the EDD and provides benefits and services to workers who are a part of a certified worker group and who are determined eligible for individual benefits and services, including: training, employment and case management services, job search and relocation allowance, and income support while attending approved training. To obtain and file a *Petition for Trade Adjustment Assistance* (ETA 9042), workers may visit the U.S. Department of Labor website (dol.gov/agencies/eta/tradeact/petitioners), contact any America's Job Center of California℠, or contact the EDD TAA State Coordinator at WSB_TAA@edd.ca.gov.

For more information about the TAA program, visit the EDD's TAA webpage at (edd.ca.gov/en/Jobs_and_Training/Trade_Act).

Work Opportunity Tax Credit

The Work Opportunity Tax Credit (WOTC) is a federal tax credit available to employers for hiring individuals from certain target groups who have consistently faced significant barriers to employment.

To be considered for the tax credit, employers must submit properly completed forms to the EDD within 28 days of the employee's start date to determine if their new hire meets the eligibility criteria.

For identification of target groups and additional information, visit Work Opportunity Tax Credit (edd.ca.gov/wotc), call 1-866-593-0173 or email WOTCSupport@edd.ca.gov.

eWOTC

eWOTC is an online service to submit, view, and manage Work Opportunity Tax Credit Request for Certification applications. This system significantly increases efficiency in processing new applications and decreases the waiting period for approvals.

To take full advantage of the benefits offered by eWOTC, employers with 25 or more employees and all agents or consultants must complete a one-time eWOTC enrollment (edd.ca.gov/wotc) to be able to submit WOTC Request for Certification applications online.

Employers with 24 employees or less, and without agent or consultant representation, are also encouraged to submit new applications online through eWOTC, but they may also mail applications to the address below. Mailed applications will take longer to process.

Employment Development Department
Work Opportunity Tax Credit Authorization Center
2901 50th Street
Sacramento, CA 95817

Go Paperless!
You can view or download this guide at California Employer Guides
(edd.ca.gov/en/Payroll_Taxes/Employers_Guides).

Labor Market Information

The Labor Market Information Division (LMID) collects, analyzes, and publishes information about California's labor market and economy. Labor market information helps employers, policy makers, and researchers develop plans and make important business decisions.

What Labor Market Information Is Available Online?

To access labor market data that is of interest to employers and the business community, visit the LMID website (labormarketinfo.edd.ca.gov). Labor market information is organized by customer type. Select **LMI by Customer** to find information specific to employers' needs, such as:

- Affirmative Action and Equal Employment Opportunity Planning Information – Get population, labor force, and summary occupational information to help with developing affirmative action programs.
- Labor Market Information for Employers – Find links to wage statistics, benefits information, data for your business plans, local labor market profiles, and more.
- National Compensation Survey – A federal survey of employee salaries, wages, and benefits.
- Quarterly Census of Employment and Wages – The program serves as a near census of monthly employment and quarterly wage information at the state and county levels and provides the most detailed industry data available.
- Local Area Profiles – Find an overview of labor market information in the state or a county, including employment and unemployment, industry payroll information, wages, the consumer price index, and more.
- Employment Projections – Estimates the changes in industry and occupational employment over time resulting from industry growth, technological change, and other factors.

Information about workplace issues, including those related to benefits, meal breaks, and pay are available from the Department of Industrial Relations (dir.ca.gov).

For assistance, contact the LMID at 1-916-262-2162 or your local Labor Market Researcher (labormarketinfo.edd.ca.gov/file/resource/LMIConsultants.pdf).

Multiple Location and Function Employers

When an employer maintains a business with more than one physical location or conducts more than one business activity or function at the same location, and the second location has a total of 10 or more employees, the employer is considered to be a multiple establishment employer. A primary location is defined as the one with the highest number of employees. If your firm fits the multiple location criteria and you are not currently completing a *Multiple Worksite Report* (BLS 3020), contact the LMID's Employment and Payroll Group at 1-855-728-7973.

Note: Filing the BLS 3020 is mandatory and must be done on a quarterly basis.

The LMID mails the federal form BLS 3020 to multiple worksite business owners at the close of each quarter (for example, December 31, 2023). Employers have until the end of the following month (for example, January 31, 2024) to return the BLS 3020 form to the Employment Development Department.

How Your Industry Code Is Determined

All businesses and government organizations are assigned an industry classification code from the North American Industry Classification System (NAICS), which allows the U.S. Bureau of Labor Statistics to tabulate national and state economic data by industry. Most new employers are assigned an industry code based on their response to Section R (Industry Activity) of the *Commercial Employer Account Registration and Update Form* (DE 1). Each year, selected employers are sent an *Industry Verification Form* (BLS 3023-NVS or NVM) to verify the accuracy of their industry code and physical location address. This process is known as the Annual Refile Survey. Other employers, who have not yet been assigned an industry code, may receive an *Industry Classification Form* (BLS 3023-NCA). Answer all questions about your business and industry thoroughly when completing these forms. For additional information, call 1-800-562-3366.

Note: The BLS 3023-NVS form can be filed electronically by using the Web ID and password provided by the Bureau of Labor Statistics. To complete the form electronically, visit the Annual Refiling Survey (idcfars.bls.gov).

The Importance of Occupational Information

The LMID collects data directly from employers primarily using surveys, such as the Occupational Employment and Wage Statistics (OEWS) Survey, to learn about the occupations used by employers and the wages paid for those occupations. The OEWS program produces employment and wage estimates annually for more than 800 occupations by industry and geographic area.

Occupational information creates the basis of good decisions made by employers, job seekers, workforce and economic development professionals, educators, public program planners, and policy makers. For example:

- Employers use occupational information for salary negotiations, to project future skills needs, and to keep a competitive edge in the local community.

- Job seekers use occupational information to become better informed about the education, training, skill, and ability requirements for specific occupations thus enabling them to make better decisions when preparing and applying for desired jobs.

- Economic developers use wage data for business attraction and retention.

- Educators and trainers use occupational information to identify areas where vocational and educational programs are needed and to create or modify the curriculum to better prepare students to meet the needs of employers.

How will my information be used?

The information employers provide will be used for statistical purposes only. All identifying information for non-government establishments will be held in strict confidence to the full extent permitted by law. OEWS information is used to support education and training decisions to help build a skilled workforce.

How do I provide my information?

Reporting electronically is easy and secure. Employers can fill out our online form or upload or email a spreadsheet. Many payroll systems will produce an electronic report with the information we need; remove personally identifiable information including employee names and Social Security numbers. Data can be submitted by:

- Online: Go to idcfoews.bls.gov. Log in using your unique IDCF number

- Email: Send an electronic spreadsheet with the number of workers in each job classification along with the hourly or annual wages to OEWSCalifornia@idcfmail.bls.gov.

- Mail: Send completed form in the enclosed postage-paid envelope

- Fax: 1-916-651-5780

- Phone: 1-800-826-4896

It is extremely important that employers respond to a request for information from the LMID. Our ability to obtain information from employers about the occupations found in California is essential for the development of tools used by decision-makers throughout our economy. If you have received an OEWS Survey, or would like more information about this program, contact the EDD at 1-800-826-4896 or at LMIOccupationalSurvey@states.bls.gov.

To access occupational information, visit Labor Market Information (labormarketinfo.edd.ca.gov) and under the **LMI by Subject section**, select **Occupations** or **Wages**.

Information and Assistance by Topic

If you have any questions regarding the following topics, contact the designated agency or office.

TOPIC	DESCRIPTION	CONTACT
California Personal Income Tax (PIT) Withholding	To request the California PIT withholding tables or for information on whether payments are subject to California PIT withholding.	EDD (edd.ca.gov) Taxpayer Assistance Center: 1-888-745-3886 Outside the U.S. or Canada, call 1-916-464-3502
California Tax Service Center (CTSC)	This is a joint tax agency website. It contains tax-related information from the Employment Development Department (EDD), the Franchise Tax Board (FTB), the California Department of Tax and Fee Administration (CDTFA), and the Internal Revenue Service (IRS).	CTSC (taxes.ca.gov)
CalJOBSSM	An online labor exchange system featuring self-service options to search for jobs, build resumes, find qualified candidates for employment, and gather information on education and training programs. Employers and job seekers may contact the nearest America's Job Center of California^{SM} for additional assistance. To locate your nearest office, visit Office Locator (edd.ca.gov/Office_Locator).	CalJOBS^{SM} Employer Helpdesk Monday through Friday 8 a.m. to 4:30 p.m. (PT) Caljobsemployer@edd.ca.gov 1-877-622-4997 CalJOBS^{SM} (caljobs.ca.gov) Central Office Workforce Services Division, MIC 50 PO Box 826880 Sacramento, CA 94280-0001 Jobs and Training (edd.ca.gov/Jobs_and_Training)
Disability Insurance (DI)	DI is a component of the State Disability Insurance (SDI) program. DI provides partial wage replacement benefits to California workers who are unable to work due to a non-work-related illness, injury, or pregnancy.	EDD Disability Insurance: • English.........1-800-480-3287 • Spanish.......1-866-658-8846 TTY: 1-800-563-2441 Employer/Licensed Health Professional Help Line: 1-855-342-3645 This phone number is dedicated to employers and licensed health professionals only. EDD Disability Insurance (edd.ca.gov/en/disability/disability_insurance)
e-Services for Business	A convenient and secure method for managing your employer payroll tax account, filing most of your returns and reports, and paying tax deposits and liabilities online. Refer to page 50 for additional information.	e-Services for Business (edd.ca.gov/Payroll_Taxes/e-Services_for_Business.htm) Taxpayer Assistance Center: 1-888-745-3886

TOPIC	DESCRIPTION	CONTACT
Economic Development	The EDD Labor Market Information Division offers data on occupational wages and outlook, employment by industry, and state and local labor market.	Labor Market Information (labormarketinfo.edd.ca.gov): 1-916-262-2162
Employee Eligibility to Work	Under federal law, employers are required to verify that every individual (citizen, national, or other) whom they hire has the right to work in the U.S. The U.S. Citizenship and Immigration Services (USCIS) requires you to complete an *Employment Eligibility Verification* (Form I-9) for each person hired to verify employment eligibility.	U.S. Citizenship and Immigration Services (www.uscis.gov) Business Liaison Automated phone service: 1-800-357-2099 Request a copy of the *Handbook for Employers: Guidance for Completing Form I-9 (M-274)*.
Employer Requirements	The Taxpayer Assistance Center can answer your payroll tax questions (e.g., employee and independent contractor status, employer registration, independent contractor reporting, and new employee reporting).	Taxpayer Assistance Center (edd.ca.gov/en/payroll_taxes/Contact_Us_ About_Payroll_Taxes): 1-888-745-3886
Employer Rights During the Employment Tax Audit and Collection Process	Employer rights are protected by the Taxpayer Advocate Office during the employment tax audit and collection process. You may request assistance from this office after first attempting to resolve an issue with the EDD representative, supervisor, and office manager.	Taxpayer Advocate Service (edd.ca.gov/en/payroll_taxes/Contact_Us_ About_Payroll_Taxes) Taxpayer Advocate Office, MIC 93 PO Box 826880 Sacramento, CA 94280-0001 Toll-Free: 1-866-594-4177 Phone: 1-916-654-8957 Fax: 1-916-449-9498
Employment Development Department Website	Provides a variety of information on the EDD programs and services, forms and publications, and links to other government sites.	EDD (edd.ca.gov)
Employment Tax Rates	A *Notice of Contribution Rates and Statement of UI Reserve Account* (DE 2088) is mailed annually by December 31 to notify employers of their UI and ETT tax rates. For additional information, refer to page 81. Protests to the DE 2088 must be submitted within 60 days of the "issued date" on the notice.	EDD Rate Management Group, MIC 4 PO Box 826880 Sacramento, CA 94280-0001 Phone: 1-916-653-7795 (24-hour automated phone system)
Employment Training Panel	Provides employers funding to train and retain workers in targeted industries in performance-based contracts. Includes retraining current employees, training new hires (unemployed individuals), and Special Employment Training program. For additional information, refer to page 97.	Employment Training Panel (etp.ca.gov) Sacramento Central Office 1-916-327-5640 **Regional Offices:** North Hollywood 1-818-755-1313 Sacramento 1-916-327-5439 San Diego 1-619-881-1777 San Francisco Bay Area 1-650-655-6930

TOPIC	DESCRIPTION	CONTACT
Federal Tax Requirements	For federal employment tax and personal income tax requirements, contact the Internal Revenue Service (IRS). The federal *Employer's Tax Guide* (Publication 15, Circular E) and *Employer's Supplemental Tax Guide* (Publication 15-A) are available from the IRS.	Internal Revenue Service (irs.gov): 1-800-829-4933
Federal Unemployment Tax Act (FUTA) Certification	The method the IRS uses to verify with the states that the credit claimed on the Form 940 or Form 1040, Schedule H, was actually paid to the state. Refer to page 82 for additional information.	EDD FUTA Certification Unit Phone: 1-916-654-8545
Forms • **Alternate Tax Forms**	The requirements and approval for using alternate forms to file your payroll tax reports can be obtained by contacting the alternate forms coordinator.	EDD Alternate Forms Coordinator 1-916-255-0649
• **Tax Forms and Publications**	Tax forms and publications are available on the Internet and Employment Tax Offices.	EDD Forms and Publications (edd.ca.gov/payroll_taxes/forms_and_publications.htm) Less than 25 copies: 1-888-745-3886 25 copies or more: 1-916-322-2835
Job Referral and Recruitment Services	The EDD Workforce Services offers a variety of services that bring employers with job openings together with qualified job seekers.	America's Job Center of California℠ (edd.ca.gov/Office_Locator). Employer Information: (edd.ca.gov/Jobs_and_Training/Employer_Information.htm)
Labor Law Requirements	Information about workplace issues, including those related to benefits, meal breaks, and pay are available on the DIR website.	Department of Industrial Relations (dir.ca.gov)
Labor Market Information	California's labor market information can help with important business decisions. Data available includes occupational employment and wage data, industry employment, labor force, and selected population characteristics.	Labor Market Information Division (labormarketinfo.edd.ca.gov): 1-916-262-2162
Paid Family Leave (PFL)	PFL is a component of the State Disability Insurance (SDI) program. PFL provides partial wage replacement benefits to California workers who take time off work to care for a seriously ill child, parent, parent-in-law, grandparent, grandchild, sibling, spouse, or registered domestic partner. Benefits are available to new parents who need time off work to bond with a new child through birth, adoption, or foster care placement. Benefits are also available to eligible workers who take time off work to participate in a qualifying event because of a spouse, registered domestic partner, parent, or child's military deployment to a foreign country.	EDD Paid Family Leave: • English............. 1-877-238-4373 • Spanish .... 1-877-379-3819 • Cantonese .... 1-866-692-5595 • Vietnamese ..... 1-866-692-5596 • Armenian .... 1-866-627-1567 • Punjabi .... 1-866-627-1568 • Tagalog............ 1-866-627-1569 TTY: 1-800-445-1312 Employer Licensed Health Professional Help Line:1-855-342-3645 This phone number is dedicated to employers and licensed health professionals only. EDD Paid Family Leave (edd.ca.gov/disability/paid_family_leave.htm)

TOPIC	DESCRIPTION	CONTACT
Payroll Tax Seminars	Seminar topics include reporting requirements, how to complete payroll tax forms, and independent contractor and employee issues.	EDD Taxpayer Assistance Center: 1-888-745-3886 Register online at EDD Payroll Tax Seminars (edd.ca.gov/payroll_tax_seminars).
Reimbursable Method of Paying Unemployment Insurance (UI) Benefits	Public employers and certain nonprofit organizations have the option of becoming "reimbursable" employers. Employers using this method to pay UI benefits are required to reimburse the UI Fund on a dollar-for-dollar basis for all UI benefits paid to their former employees.	EDD Reimbursable Accounting Group, MIC 19 PO Box 826880 Sacramento, CA 94280 1-916-653-5846
School Employees Fund (SEF)	Only California public school employers (kindergarten through 12th grade), California community colleges, and charter schools may elect to participate in the SEF (UI program) to finance UI benefits.	EDD School Employees Fund, MIC 13 PO Box 826880 Sacramento, CA 94280 1-916-653-5380 School Employees Fund (edd.ca.gov/en/Payroll_Taxes/School_ Employees_Fund)
Small Business Assistance Center	Located on the California Tax Service Center website, it provides helpful information about starting, running, or closing your business.	California Tax Service Center (taxes.ca.gov)
State Disability Insurance (SDI) Program	SDI program provides two benefits: Disability Insurance (DI) and Paid Family Leave (PFL). DI provides partial wage replacement benefits to California workers who are unable to work due to a non-work-related illness, injury, or pregnancy. PFL provides partial wage replacement benefits to California workers who take time off work to care for a seriously ill family member, to bond with a new child, or to participate in a qualifying event because of a family member's military deployment to a foreign country. The SDI program is funded through employee payroll deductions.	EDD Disability Insurance: • English.............1-800-480-3287 • Spanish ....1-866-658-8846 Hearing Impaired (TTY): 1-800-563-2441 EDD Paid Family Leave: • English.............1-877-238-4373 • Spanish ....1-877-379-3819 • Cantonese ....1-877-692-5595 • Vietnamese .....1-866-692-5596 • Armenian ....1-866-627-1567 • Punjabi ....1-866-627-1568 • Tagalog............1-866-627-1569 TTY: 1-800-445-1312 Employer/Licensed Health Professional Help Line: 1-855-342-3645 This phone number is dedicated to employers and licensed health professional only. EDD State Disability Insurance (edd.ca.gov/disability).

TOPIC	DESCRIPTION	CONTACT
SDI Online	SDI Online is our electronic claim filing system available to employees and licensed health professionals, for submission of Disability Insurance (DI) and Paid Family Leave (PFL) claim information. Employers, Voluntary Plan (VP) employers, and third-party administrators can use SDI online to securely submit employee information for DI claims online.	EDD SDI Online Employer/Licensed Health Professional Help Line: 1-855-342-3645 This phone number is dedicated to employers and licensed health professionals only. SDI Online (edd.ca.gov/disability/SDI_online.htm) VP VPProgram@edd.ca.gov
State Information Data Exchange System (SIDES)	SIDES is a secure and timely way for employers and third party administrators to electronically receive and respond to the EDD's *Notice of Unemployment Insurance Claim Filed* (DE 1101CZ). SIDES streamlines communication to help employers manage their UI account and reduce improper payments.	EDD SIDES E-Response Technical Support: 1-855-327-7057 SIDES Web Service Technical Support SIDES-support@naswa.org This number is for employers with inquiries related specifically to SIDES. Employers with questions about the Unemployment Insurance (UI) program should use the phone numbers listed below under Unemployment Insurance Benefits.
Tax Debt – California Payroll Taxes • **Offers in Compromise**	Enables a qualified tax debtor to eliminate an employment tax liability at less than full value.	EDD Offers in Compromise: 1-916-464-2739
• **Settlements Program**	Provides employers and the state an opportunity to avoid the cost of prolonged litigation associated with resolving disputed employment tax issues.	EDD Settlements Office, MIC 93 PO Box 826880 Sacramento, CA 94280-0001 Phone: 1-916-653-9130 Fax: 1-916-449-2161
Taxpayer Assistance Center	For general tax information, the Taxpayer Assistance Center staff is available 8 a.m. to 5 p.m., PT, Monday through Friday. The Taxpayer Assistance Center will be closed on state holidays.	EDD Taxpayer Assistance Center: 1-888-745-3886 Outside the U.S. or Canada, call 1-916-464-3502 TTY: 1-800-547-9565
Taxpayer Advocate Office	If you are unable to resolve an employment tax problem with an EDD representative, supervisor, and office manager, you can contact the Taxpayer Advocate Office for assistance.	Taxpayer Advocate Office (edd.ca.gov/payroll_taxes/taxpayer_advocate.htm) Taxpayer Advocate Office, MIC 93 PO Box 826880 Sacramento, CA 94280-0001 Toll-Free: 1-866-594-4177 Phone: 1-916-654-8957 Fax: 1-916-449-9498
Underground Economy	Investigates businesses that are paying workers undocumented cash payments or not complying with labor, taxes, and licensing laws.	Underground Economy Operations (edd.ca.gov/en/Payroll_Taxes/Underground_Economy_Operations) 1-800-528-1783 ueo@edd.ca.gov

TOPIC	DESCRIPTION	CONTACT
Unemployment Insurance (UI) Benefits	Provides temporary income to unemployed workers who meet the UI eligibility requirements.	EDD Unemployment Insurance Services **Phone** • English and Spanish......1-800-300-5616 • Armenian ....1-855-528-1518 • Cantonese ....1-800-547-3506 • Korean..........................1-844-660-0877 • Vietnamese ....1-800-547-2058 • Mandarin ....1-866-303-0706 • Tagalog.........................1-866-395-1513 Hearing Impaired (TTY).....1-800-815-9387 UI program self-service......1-866-333-4606 **Employer Information:** Employers who call should listen to the introduction message, select language choice, and press *5* for the employer menu (available in English and Spanish) that provides UI and Workforce Service information, or visit Unemployment (edd.ca.gov/unemployment) and select the Employer Information link (edd.ca.gov/unemployment). **Claimant Information:** File for UI benefits using one of the following methods: • **Online:** UI Online^{SM} is the fastest and most convenient way to file your UI claim. Visit UI Online^{SM} (edd.ca.gov/en/unemployment/ui_online) to get started. • **Phone:** Call one of the phone numbers listed above and speak with an EDD representative 8 a.m. to 12 noon (PT). Monday to Friday, except on state holidays. • **Fax or Mail:** When filing a new claim through UI Online^{SM}, some customers will be instructed to fax or mail their UI application to the EDD. If this occurs, the paper *Unemployment Insurance Application* (DE 1101I) will display. For faster and more secure processing, fax the completed form to the number listed on the form. If you decide to mail your UI application, use the address on the form and allow additional time for processing.

TOPIC	DESCRIPTION	CONTACT
Unemployment Insurance Benefit Charges	A *Statement of Charges to Reserve Account* (DE 428T) is mailed annually in September. This statement is an itemized list of UI charges to your reserve account. For additional information, refer to page 93. Protests to the DE 428T must be submitted within 60 days of the **issued date** on the notice.	EDD Contribution Rate Group, MIC 4 PO Box 826831 Sacramento, CA 94320-6831 1-916-653-7795 (24-hour automated phone system)
Voluntary Plan	California law allows an employer to apply to the EDD for approval of a Voluntary Plan (VP) for the payment of Disability Insurance (DI) and Paid Family Leave (PFL) benefits in place of the mandatory State Disability Insurance (SDI) state plan. A VP must provide all the benefits of SDI, at least one benefit that is better than SDI, and it cannot cost employees more than SDI. Once a VP is approved, an employer is no longer required to send SDI withholdings to the EDD. Instead, the employer holds the contributions in a separate trust fund to pay the DI and PFL benefits and approved expenses.	EDD Voluntary Plan (edd.ca.gov/disability/Employer_Voluntary_Plans.htm) 1-916-653-6839
Workers' Compensation Insurance	If you have employees, you are required by law to have workers' compensation insurance coverage. Failure to do so is a crime and may result in penalties and closure of your business.	Workers' Compensation Insurance (dir.ca.gov/dwc) Your insurance agent or Division of Workers' Compensation 1-800-736-7401
Workforce Services	The EDD offers a variety of services that brings employers with job openings together with qualified job seekers.	Find a local EDD office or America's Job Center of California^{SM} (edd.ca.gov/Office_Locator).
Work Opportunity Tax Credit (WOTC)	The EDD is the WOTC certifying agency for California employers. WOTC promotes the hiring of individuals who qualify as a member of a target group and provides a federal tax credit to employers who hire these individuals.	EDD Work Opportunity Tax Credit (edd.ca.gov/Jobs_and_Training/Work_Opportunity_Tax_Credit.htm) 1-866-593-0173 WOTCSupport@edd.ca.gov

For the latest tax news and employer resources, visit
California Employer News and Updates
(edd.ca.gov/payroll_taxes/employer-news.htm).

Subscribe to the EDD no-cost email subscription services
(edd.ca.gov/about_edd/get_email_notices.htm).

Glossary

Automated Clearing House (ACH) – Any entity that operates as a clearing house for electronic debit or credit transactions pursuant to an Electronic Funds Transfer agreement with an association that is a member of the National ACH Association.

Base Period – The base period consists of four calendar quarters of three months each. When a base period begins and which calendar quarters are used depends on what date the claim begins and whether the claim is for Unemployment Insurance (UI) or for State Disability Insurance (SDI). For UI, there are two types of base periods: the Standard Base Period (see Base Period, Standard [UI]) and Alternate Base Period (see Base Period, Alternate [UI]). The Alternate Base Period can **only** be used to file a UI claim when there are not enough wages earned in the Standard Base Period to file a monetarily valid UI claim. For SDI, a base period covers 12 months and is divided into 4 consecutive quarters. The base period includes wages subject to SDI tax which were paid approximately 5 to 18 months before the claim start date.

Base Period, Alternate (UI) – The UI Alternate Base Period is the last four completed calendar quarters prior to the beginning date of the claim. The Alternate Base Period can only be used if an individual cannot monetarily establish a valid UI claim using the Standard Base Period.

Base Period Employer – Employers who paid the earnings used to establish a UI claim and calculate an award.

Base Period, Standard (UI) – The UI Standard Base Period is the first four of the last five completed calendar quarters prior to the beginning date of the claim.

CCR – The California Code of Regulations (govt.westlaw.com/calregs).

CUIAB – The California Unemployment Insurance Appeals Board (cuiab.ca.gov).

California Unemployment Insurance Code (CUIC) – The laws administering California's Unemployment Insurance (UI), Employment Training Tax (ETT), State Disability Insurance (SDI), and Personal Income Tax programs (PIT). The CUIC is available at (leginfo.legislature.ca.gov/faces/codes.xhtml).

Cash Wages – Checks, currency, and electronic debit payments paid to employees.

Charges – Amounts deducted from an employer's reserve account or amounts reimbursable for state UI benefits paid to former employees.

Claim – An application for Unemployment Insurance (UI), Disability Insurance (DI), or Paid Family Leave (PFL) benefits.

> UI – The process that establishes a UI benefit year is called a new claim. *Weekly Continued Claim* (DE 4581) forms are used by claimants to certify for UI benefits during the benefit year. The EDD has two additional methods that unemployed individuals may use to certify for UI benefits. Rather than filling out and submitting a paper DE 4581 by mail, EDD Tele-Cert allows individuals to certify for benefits using the phone and EDD UI Online allows individuals to certify for UI benefits through the EDD website. After establishing a benefit year, claimants can interrupt their claims for a variety of reasons. For example, the claimant may receive a disqualification, obtain intervening employment, or fail to continue to certify for benefits. The claimant may request to reopen an existing claim with a claim balance during the benefit year.

> DI – The application that establishes a DI benefit period is called an initial claim. Subsequent certifications on that DI claim are called continued claims. For each separate period of disability, a new first initial claim must be filed.

> PFL – The application that establishes a PFL benefit period is called an initial claim. Subsequent certifications on that claim are called continued claims. For each separate period of family leave, an initial claim must be filed.

Claimant – A California wage-earner who files a claim for UI, DI, or PFL benefits.

Contributions – Employer's payroll tax payments for UI and ETT. The CUIC refers to taxes under its provision as "Contributions." In this guide, "Contributions" are generally referred to as "Taxes."

Glossary

Deposit – An amount of money electronically submitted to the EDD with a *Payroll Tax Deposit* (DE 88) through the e-Services for Business (edd.ca.gov/eServices). For additional information, refer to page 57.

Determination – A decision regarding a claimant's eligibility to receive UI, DI, or PFL benefits.

Disability Insurance (DI) – Benefits paid to eligible California workers who have a loss of wages when they are unable to work due to a non-work-related illness, injury, or pregnancy. DI is a component of the State Disability Insurance (SDI) program and funded through employee payroll deductions.

Electronic Funds Transfer (EFT) – An electronic method of remitting state payroll tax payments. Funds are transferred from your bank account (with payment information) to the state's account.

Employee – A wage-earner in employment covered by the CUIC.

Employer Payroll Tax Account Number – The Employment Development Department (EDD) eight-digit employer payroll tax account number assigned to each registered employer (e.g., 000-0000-0). Always refer to your EDD employer payroll tax account number when communicating with the EDD. Omission of your employer payroll tax account number may result in delays in processing payments, reporting documents, and correspondence.

Employment Taxes – Unemployment Insurance (UI) Tax, Employment Training Tax (ETT), State Disability Insurance (SDI) Tax, and Personal Income Tax (PIT) withholding.

Employment Training Fund – A special fund in the State Treasury for depositing into or transferring all ETT contributions collected from employers.

Employment Training Panel (ETP) – Administers the employment training funds that are provided by the ETT to train and retain workers with job skills needed by employers. Funds may be used to train unemployed individuals or to train and retain current workers of businesses, primarily businesses facing out-of-state competition.

Employment Training Tax (ETT) – An employer-paid tax that funds jobs skills training for employees in targeted industries to improve the competitiveness of California businesses. Employers subject to ETT pay one-tenth of one percent (.001) of the first $7,000 in wages paid to each employee per year.

E-file and E-pay Mandate – State law requires all employers to electronically submit employment tax returns, wage reports, and payroll tax deposits to the EDD. Beginning January 1, 2018, all employers became subject to this requirement.

e-Services for Business – Online tool that allows employers to manage their employer payroll tax accounts online. New employers can register for an EDD employer payroll tax account number online. Registered employers can access account and payment information, file most returns and reports, including New Employee Registry (NER) and Independent Contractor Reporting (ICR), pay tax deposits and tax liabilities, review statements, correspondence, and email messages, obtain tax rates, change addresses, make payment arrangements, close and/or reopen their account. For additional information about the EDD e-Services for Business, refer to page 50.

Excluded Employment – Employment specifically excluded from coverage pursuant to the CUIC.

Experience Rating – The system by which an employer's UI contribution rate is determined each calendar year based on previous employment experience.

Good Cause – A substantial reason that provides a legal basis for an employer filing a tax report or submitting a late payment. *Good Cause* cannot exist unless there are unusual circumstances or circumstances that could not be reasonably foreseen, for example, earthquakes or floods. For more information, contact the Taxpayer Assistance Center at 1-888-745-3886.

Household Employment – Describes employment of a household nature.

Glossary

Independent Contractor – An independent contractor (service-provider) is any individual who is not an employee of the service-recipient for California purposes and who receives compensation or executes a contract for services performed for that business or government entity in or outside of California. Refer to page 8 for Independent Contractor determination reference material. For additional information about filing the *Report of Independent Contractor(s)* (DE 542), refer to page 55.

Interstate Benefit Audit – Each quarter, the EDD runs a cross-match with wages earned in other states against California's Unemployment Insurance Benefits paid file. When the crossmatch identifies an overlap between the earnings reported by the out-of-state employers and weeks the claimant was paid UI benefits, the system automatically generates the *Interstate Unemployment Insurance Benefit Payment Audit* (IB 8605) that is mailed to the out-of-state employer(s).

Labor Market Information (LMI) – California's labor market information can help in making important business decisions. Data available includes occupational employment and wage data, industry employment, labor force, occupation and industry projections of employment, and selected population characteristics.

Mid-month Employment – The number of full-time and part-time employees who worked during or received pay subject to UI for the payroll period that includes the 12th day of the month.

Multiple Establishment Employer – An employer that maintains a business at more than one physical location and/or conducts more than one business activity/function at the same location and the secondary locations have a total of 10 or more employees.

New Employee Registry (NER) – California's new hire reporting program. Employers are required to report their new or rehired employees within 20 days of their start-of-work date. Refer to *Report of New Employee(s)* (DE 34) on page 53.

North American Industry Classification System (NAICS) – The six-digit industry classification code that identifies the primary business functions of an employer's business. Visit the United States Census Bureau (census.gov/naics/) for more information.

Paid Family Leave (PFL) – Benefits paid to eligible California workers who take time off work to care for a seriously ill family member, to bond with a new child, or to participate in a qualifying event because of a family member's military deployment to a foreign country. PFL is a component of the State Disability Insurance program and is funded through employee payroll deductions.

Payroll Period – The frequency you pay wages: daily, weekly, bi-weekly (every two weeks), semi-monthly (twice a month), etc.

Payroll Records – Records providing an accurate account of all workers (employed, laid off, on a leave of absence, or an independent contractor) and all payments made.

Payroll Taxes (State) – Unemployment Insurance (UI) Tax, Employment Training Tax (ETT), State Disability Insurance (SDI) Tax, and Personal Income Tax (PIT) withholding.

Personal Income Tax (PIT) Wages – All wages paid during the periods that are subject to PIT, even if they are not subject to PIT withholding. The PIT wages consist of all compensation for services by employees for their employer and include, but are not limited to, salaries, fees, bonuses, commissions, and payments in forms other than cash or checks. Wages in any form other than cash or checks are measured by the fair market value of the goods, lodging, meals, or other compensation given in payment for the employee's services. The calendar year total for PIT wages should agree with the amount reported on the individual's *Wage and Tax Statement* (Form W-2), in Box 16 (State Wages, Tips, etc.).

Personal Income Tax (PIT) Withholding – California PIT is withheld from employees' pay based on the *Employee's Withholding Allowance Certificate* (DE 4) on file with the employer.

Predecessor – A previous owner registered with the EDD as an employer.

Prepayments (UI and ETT) – UI or ETT taxes that an employer voluntarily sends to the EDD during a quarter even though they are not due until the end of the quarter.

Glossary

Registered Domestic Partner – A domestic partnership registered with the Secretary of State in California pursuant to section 297 of the Family Code.

Reimbursable Employer – A public entity employer or certain types of nonprofit employers who are permitted by law to be billed for UI benefits after they are paid to former employees.

Reserve Account – A book account kept for each tax-rated employer to measure employment experience and set the employer's UI tax rate.

Ruling on Benefit Claim – For tax-rated employers, a ruling is the EDD decision as to whether an employer's reserve account will be charged for UI benefits. The ruling is based on the reason for separation.

Ruling on Tax Question – A decision, in writing, as to an employer's subject status or tax liability in the stated circumstances.

School Employees Fund (SEF) – A UI financing method available only to California public schools (kindergarten through 12th grade), California community colleges, and charter schools.

SDI Online – An electronic claim filing system available to individuals filing for benefits and licensed health professionals for submission of Disability Insurance (DI) and Paid Family Leave (PFL) claim information. Employers, Voluntary Plan employers and third-party administrators can use SDI Online to securely submit employee information (e.g., wages earned, last day worked, etc.) for DI claims.

Service-Provider – An individual (independent contractor) who is not an employee of the service-recipient for California purposes and who receives compensation or executes a contract for services performed for that business or government entity in or outside of California.

Service-Recipient – Any business or government entity that, for California purposes, pays compensation to a service-provider (independent contractor) or executes a contract for services to be performed by an independent contractor in or outside of California.

Settlement Date – The date an electronic payment transaction is completed and posted on the books of the Federal Reserve Bank and the state's bank account.

SIDES – State Information Data Exchange System allows employers and third-party administrators to electronically receive and respond to the EDD's *Notice of Unemployment Claim Filed* (DE 1101CZ).

Social Security Number (SSN) – A nine-digit number issued to an individual by the Social Security Administration. All employee wage records and claim actions are filed under this number, rather than by name.

State Disability Insurance (SDI) – The SDI program provides Disability Insurance (DI) and Paid Family Leave (PFL) benefits to eligible workers who need time off work because of disability or family leave. DI benefits are paid to eligible California workers who have a loss of wages when they are unable to work due to an illness, injury, or pregnancy. PFL benefits are paid to eligible California workers who take time off work to care for a seriously ill family member, to bond with a new child, or to participate in a qualifying event because of a family member's military deployment to a foreign country. The SDI program is funded by mandatory payroll deductions from employee wages.

Subject Employer – An employer who is liable pursuant to the rules and provisions of the CUIC.

Subject Quarter – The calendar quarter when an employer first meets the requirements for reporting their payroll taxes.

Subject Wages – Subject wages are used to determine UI, DI, and PFL benefits. Generally, all wages are considered subject wages regardless of the UI and SDI taxable wage limits. Refer to the inside front cover of this guide for current rates and taxable wage limits. For special classes of employment and payments that may not be considered subject wages, refer to *Information Sheet: Types of Employment* (DE 231TE) and *Information Sheet: Types of Payments* (DE 231TP).

Successor – A change in ownership or a new ownership of a business already registered with the EDD as an employer.

Tax-Rated Employer – An employer who is required to register with the EDD and pay UI taxes each year on wages paid to each of their employees, up to the UI taxable wage limit.

Glossary

Tax Return – A *Quarterly Contribution Return and Report of Wages* (DE 9) or an *Employer of Household Workers Annual Payroll Tax Return* (DE 3HW). Quarterly household employers are required to file a tax return each quarter to reconcile California payroll tax payments and the total subject wages reported. Annual household employers are required to file the tax return annually.

Taxable Wage Limit – The maximum amount of an employee's wages that certain taxes apply to in a calendar year. Refer to the inside front cover of this publication for taxable wage limits.

Taxable Wages – Compensation paid for *covered employment* up to the applicable taxable wage limits for the year. Compensation includes wages and allowances such as meals, lodging, and other payments in lieu of money for services rendered in employment.

Unemployment Insurance (UI) – Benefits paid to eligible California workers who are unemployed. Recipients must meet specific qualifications to receive benefits. UI is funded by employer payroll taxes.

Voluntary Plan (VP) – California law allows an employer to apply to the EDD for approval of a VP for the payment of DI and PFL benefits in place of the mandatory SDI state plan. A VP must provide all the benefits of SDI, at least one benefit that is better than SDI, and it cannot cost employees more than SDI. Once a VP is approved, an employer is no longer required to send SDI withholdings to the EDD for those employees covered by the VP. Instead, if the plan is paid by employees, the employer holds the VP contributions in a separate trust fund to pay the DI or PFL benefits and approved expenses. The employer may enlist a greater benefit by paying for the plan rather than having the employees pay for it. The VP employer pays a quarterly assessment to the EDD based on the taxable wages of employees participating in the plan and other factors.

Wage Detail – A *Quarterly Contribution Return and Report of Wages (Continuation)* (DE 9C) filed each quarter listing employee(s) full name, SSN, total subject wages, PIT wages, and PIT withholding.

Wage Report – A *Quarterly Contribution Return and Report of Wages (Continuation)* (DE 9C) or an *Employer of Household Worker(s) Quarterly Report of Wages and Withholdings* (DE 3BHW). Both quarterly and annual household employers are required to file a wage report each quarter to report employee wage and payroll tax withholding information.

Wages – All payments made to employees, whether paid by check, cash, or the reasonable cash value of noncash payments, such as meals and lodging.

Work Opportunity Tax Credit (WOTC) – Federal tax credits for employers who hire and retain job seekers from any one of 10 different target groups.

Worker Adjustment and Retraining Notification (WARN) Act – Protects employees, their families, and communities by requiring that employers give a 60-day notice to the affected employees and both state and local representatives prior to a plant closing or mass layoff.

Index

Index

Index

Topic

Index

Topic

Index

Topic

Instructions for Ordering Forms and Publications

The EDD provides easy access to its forms, publications, and information sheets by phone or online on the EDD website (edd.ca.gov).

Reminder: All employers are required to electronically submit employment tax returns, wage reports, and payroll tax deposits to the Employment Development Department (EDD). Refer to page 49 for information on the e-file and e-pay mandate and related noncompliance penalties.

Go Paperless!
The *California Employer's Guide* (DE 44) (edd.ca.gov/en/Payroll_Taxes/Employers_Guides) is available online.

To go paperless, complete your Employer's Guide Mailing Preference (eddservices.edd.ca.gov/tap/open/annualguide/_/#1).

Order Forms Online
EDD Forms (edd.ca.gov/forms)

Download Forms
Online Forms and Publications (edd.ca.gov/payroll_taxes/forms_and_publications.htm)

By Phone:
For quantities of 25 or more, call 1-916-322-2835.
For quantities of 24 or less, call 1-888-745-3886.

If you require additional assistance, contact the Taxpayer Assistance Center at 1-888-745-3886.

For the latest tax news and employer resources, visit
California Employer News and Updates
(edd.ca.gov/payroll_taxes/employer-news.htm).

Subscribe to the EDD no-cost email subscription services
(edd.ca.gov/about_edd/get_email_notices.htm).

STATE OF CALIFORNIA

LABOR AND WORKFORCE DEVELOPMENT AGENCY

EMPLOYMENT DEVELOPMENT DEPARTMENT

**Employment
Development
Department**

State of California

PO Box 826880, Sacramento, CA 94280-0001

OFFICIAL BUSINESS
PENALTY FOR PRIVATE USE $300

Made in the USA
Las Vegas, NV
29 April 2024